The Anti-Inflammatory Cookbook

Delicious Recipes to Reduce Inflammation and Boost Your Health

Keri Young

Copyright © 2023 - All rights reserved.

The content contained within this book may not be reproduced, duplicated, or transmitted without direct written permission from the author or the publisher.

Under no circumstances will any blame or legal responsibility be held against the publisher, or author, for any damages, reparation, or monetary loss due to the information contained within this book. Either directly or indirectly.

Legal Notice: This book is copyright protected. This book is only for personal use. You cannot amend, distribute, sell, use, quote, or paraphrase any part, or the content within this book, without the consent of the author or publisher.

Disclaimer Notice: Please note the information contained within this document is for educational and entertainment purposes only. All effort has been executed to present accurate, up-to-date, and reliable, complete information. No warranties of any kind are declared or implied. Readers acknowledge that the author is not engaging in the rendering of legal, financial, medical, or professional advice. The content within this book has been derived from various sources. Please consult a licensed professional before attempting any techniques outlined in this book.

By reading this document, the reader agrees that under no circumstances is the author responsible for any losses, direct or indirect, which are incurred as a result of the use of the information contained within this document, including, but not limited to, — errors, omissions, or inaccuracies.

Table of Contents

Breakfast Recipes _____ 7
    Anti-Inflammatory Smoothie _____ 8
    Chamomile and Maple Porridge _____ 9
    Mexican Breakfast Hash _____ 10
    Chia Pudding _____ 12
    Homemade Muesli _____ 13
    Fresh Turmeric Smoothie Bowl _____ 15
    Sweet Potato Toasts _____ 16
    Southwest Tofu Scramble _____ 17
    Baby Kale Breakfast Salad with Quinoa & Strawberries ___ 19
    Parsley Frittata _____ 20
    Oatmeal with Turmeric Powder _____ 21
    Zucchini Oatmeal _____ 22

Appetizer Recipes _____ 23
    Sweet Potato Soup _____ 24
    Broccoli with garlic and lemon _____ 26
    Quinoa and Vegetable Soup _____ 27
    Beet Hummus _____ 29
    Asparagus & Snap Pea Salad with Crispy Prosciutto _____ 30
    Tomato & Greens Salad _____ 32
    Oatmeal Crackers _____ 33
    Grilled Eggplant Provolone _____ 35
    Vegan Kimchi _____ 36
    Mixed Fruit Salad _____ 38
    Grilled Tomatoes _____ 39
    Beet Salad _____ 40
    Winter Orange & Fennel Salad _____ 41
    Parsley Sauce _____ 42
    Celery Root Salad _____ 43

Meat Recipes — 44
- Chicken, Avocado & Quinoa Bowls with Herb Dressing — 45
- White Bean and Chicken Chili Blanca — 47
- Roasted Chicken With Balsamic Vinaigrette — 48
- Sweet & Sour Chicken — 50
- Pulled Pork — 52
- Turkey Shepherd's Pie — 53
- Cheesy Broccoli Chicken Rice — 55

Seafood Recipes — 56
- Blackened Salmon — 57
- Garlic Shrimp and Asparagus with Zucchini Noodles — 58
- Superfood Baked Salmon — 59
- Roasted Salmon, Smoky Chickpeas, and Greens — 61
- Sheet Pan Turmeric Salmon With Cherry Sauce — 63
- Creamy Sundried Tomato Pan Seared Sole — 65
- Fish Ceviche — 66
- Thai Green Curry with Shrimp and Kale — 68

Vegetable Recipes — 70
- Vegan Roasted Pumpkin Curry — 71
- Ratatouille — 73
- Carrot Ginger Soup — 75
- Curry Tofu — 77
- Cumin Zucchini Rings — 78
- Instant Pot Potato Leek Soup — 79
- Broccoli Soup — 81
- Sorrel Soup — 82

Main Courses Meat Recipes — 83
- Slow Cooker Dairy-Free Butter Chicken — 84
- Grilled Curry Chicken — 86
- Beefy Bake Casserole — 87
- Kung Pao Chicken — 88
- Chicken piccata with garlicky greens & new potatoes — 90
- Apple Cider Vinegar Chicken — 92

Boiled Chicken	93
Vegetable Recipes II	**94**
Curried Chickpea Lettuce Wraps	95
Mediterranean Grilled Eggplant Salad	97
Red Beet Borscht	99
Stir-Fried Asparagus with Bell Peppers and Cashew Nuts	101
Vegan Tacos	103
Sweet Potatoes with Swiss Chard	105
Stuffed Peppers	106
Sautéed greens with fennel	107
Desserts	**108**
Pumpkin Balls	109
Mango Pudding	110
Strawberry Shortbreads	111
Gingerbread Dessert Hummus	112
Watermelon Pizza	113
Chocolate Avocado Pudding	114
Apple Chips	115
Pineapple Sorbet	116
Kiwi Sorbet	117
Fresh Fig & Banana Smoothie	118
Almond Butter Avocado Fudgsicles	119
Easy Roasted Fruit	121
Guava Smoothie	122
Orange Ginger Turmeric Smoothie	123
Turmeric Apple Cider Ginger Gummies	124
Herbal Teas	**125**
Peppermint Tea	126
Almond Tea	127
Chamomile Tea	128
Turmeric Tea	129
Herbal Tea	130
Lemon Grass Tea	131

Peach Tea	132
Jasmine Tea	133
Herbs	**134**
Italian Seasoning	135
All-Purpose No-Salt Seasoning Mix	136
Garlic-Herb Seasoning	137
Poultry Seasoning	138
Anti-Inflammatory Oil	139
Sambal Oelek	140
Hot Ketchup	141
Mustard Dressing	142
Measuring Conversions	**143**

Breakfast Recipes

Anti-Inflammatory Smoothie

Preparation time: 5 minutes | Total time: 50 minutes

Servings: 2 | Difficulty Level: Easy

Nutritional Information:

Calories: 326 Kcal, Protein: 8 g, Carbohydrates: 61 g, Fat: 10 g, Fiber: 10 g

Ingredients:

- 1 teaspoon of fresh Turmeric; peeled & grated
- 2 cups of ripe strawberries; chopped & frozen
- 1 teaspoon of fresh ginger; peeled & grated
- 1/2 cup of orange juice
- 2/3 cup of beet; roasted, chopped & frozen
- 1 cup of unsweetened almond milk

Options for serving:

- Goji berries
- Full-fat coconut milk
- Raw cashews

Instructions:

1. Cut beets into chunks measuring 1/2", wrapped with foil, then bake for 45 to 50 mins at 400 degrees F. The beet may be cut in half and steamed for 20 minutes or until it yields to a fork prick test. After cooking your beet, let it cool, then put it in the freezer for two hours. Because you may need 2/3 cup, you could have leftover roasted beet that you can use in salads. Blend all the ingredients in a blender until they are perfectly smooth. Serve with goji berries and full-fat coconut milk.

Chamomile and Maple Porridge

Preparation time: 5 minutes | Total time: 15 minutes

Servings: 1 | Difficulty Level: Easy

Nutritional Information:

Calories: 398 Kcal, Protein: 10 g, Carbohydrates: 46 g, Fat: 21 g, Fiber: 2 g

Ingredients:

- 1 tablespoon of coconut butter
- Scant 1 cup of plant-based milk (cashew milk)
- 1 teaspoon of maple syrup
- 2 teaspoons of dried chamomile flowers
- 1/2 cup of rolled oats
- 1 tablespoon of flax seeds /chia seeds
- Sliced almonds; toasted (for garnish)

Instructions:

1. Combine the oats, a scant 1/2 cup (115ml) of boiling water, and the plant-based milk in a sizeable saucepan over low heat. Add chamomile tea leaves or flowers. Cook while stirring continuously for 10 minutes. Remove any bigger flower pieces if desired. Add the almond slices, maple syrup, coconut butter, and flax or chia seeds as garnishes.

Mexican Breakfast Hash

Preparation time: 10 minutes | Total time: 45 minutes

Servings: 4 | Difficulty Level: Easy

Nutritional Information:

Calories: 518 Kcal, Protein: 32 g, Carbohydrates: 27 g, Fat: 31g, Fiber: 6 g

Ingredients:

- 3 Sweet Potatoes; large dice
- 2 tsp of Poultry Seasoning
- 1 Jalapeno Pepper; minced
- 2 Poblano peppers; small dice
- 1 tbsp of Fennel Seed
- 2 tsp of Minced Garlic
- 1 pound of Ground pork
- 1/2 Red Onion; small dice
- 1 tsp of Cumin
- 2 tsp of Chili Powder
- 2 tbsp of Avocado Oil
- 1 tsp of Smoked Paprika
- 1/4 cup of Fresh Cilantro chopped
- Salt/Pepper; to taste
- 1 Lime; wedges

Instructions:

1. Set your oven to 400 degrees F. Sweet potatoes are diced into bite-sized pieces and tossed with 1 tablespoon of oil. Place on a baking sheet and cook in the oven for 30 to 40 minutes, stirring halfway through.
2. In a big skillet, warm the remaining oil over medium-high heat. Before adding garlic, peppers, onion, and spices sauté the ground pork with the poultry seasoning and fennel for

approximately 5 minutes.
3. Cook the meat and veggies together in a pan until they are tender. Top roasted sweet potatoes with meat mixture, cilantro, and lime.

Chia Pudding

Preparation time: 15 minutes | Total time: 45 minutes

Servings: 4 | Difficulty Level: Easy

Nutritional Information:

Calories: 187 Kcal, Protein: 9 g, Carbohydrates: 11 g, Fat: 12 g, Fiber: 8 g

Ingredients:

- 4 oz Soft Tofu
- 1 cup of blueberries
- 375 ml Almond Milk; Almond Breeze
- 1/4 cup of Sliced Almonds
- 1/2 tsp of Pure Almond Extract
- 1/4 cup of Chia Seeds

Instructions:

1. Combine tofu, almond milk, and extract in a blender (or food processor). Blend until the mixture is smooth and thoroughly blended. Transfer to a bowl, mix in the chia seeds, and set aside for 10 minutes.
2. Heat a small pan over low-medium heat, add the almond slices, and constantly stir until they are gently toasted.
3. Remove the pan from the heat and put it aside. Add blueberries to the chia seed mixture gently. Chia pudding should be refrigerated before serving.
4. Distribute equally among four small dishes; if preferred, top with the toasted almonds and more blueberries.

Homemade Muesli

Preparation time: 15 minutes | Total Time: 15 minutes

Servings: 8 | Difficulty Level: Medium

Nutritional Information:

Calories: 275 kcal, Protein: 8.5 g, Carbohydrates: 36.4 g, Fat: 13 g, Fiber: 7.5 g

Ingredients:

- 1/2 cup of wheat bran
- 3 1/2 cups of rolled oats
- 1/2 teaspoon of ground cinnamon
- 1/2 teaspoon of kosher salt
- 1/4 cup of raw pecans: coarsely chopped
- 1/2 cup of sliced almonds
- 1/2 cup of unsweetened coconut flakes
- 1/4 cup of raw pepitas: (shelled pumpkin seeds)
- 1/4 cup of dried cherries
- 1/4 cup of dried apricots: coarsely chopped

Instructions:

1. Grain, nuts, and seeds are lightly toasted. Heat an oven to 350°F and split it into thirds using two racks. On a rimmed baking sheet, mix the salt, wheat bran, oats, and cinnamon; toss to blend and distribute into an equal layer. On a second rimmed baking sheet, add the almonds, pecans, and pepitas; toss them and distribute them into an equal layer. Place the oats on the top rack and the nuts on the bottom rack in the oven. Bake for 10 to 12 minutes or until nuts are aromatic.
2. Toss in the coconut. Take the baking sheet with nuts out of the oven and put it aside to cool. Sprinkle the coconut over the oats, return to the top rack, and bake for another 5 minutes or until the coconut is golden brown. Remove them from the

oven and put them aside for 10 minutes to cool.
3. Place them in a large mixing bowl. Add dried fruit to the mix. Toss in the cherries and apricots to combine. Place the contents in an airtight container. Muesli may be kept at room temperature for up to a month in an airtight container.
4. Enjoy as you want. Serve with fresh fruit and a sprinkle of honey or maple syrup, like overnight oats, oatmeal, cereal, or yogurt.

Fresh Turmeric Smoothie Bowl

Total Time: 0 minutes | Preparation time: 5 minutes

Servings: 6 | Difficulty Level: Medium

Nutritional Information:

Calories: 24 kcal, protein: 8 g, carbohydrates: 15 g, Fat: 25 g, Fiber: 7 g

Ingredients:

- 1 orange
- 1 cup of frozen mango
- 1/2 lemon
- 1 cup of frozen cauliflower
- 1 tbsp of coconut oil
- 1-inch piece of fresh Turmeric
- 1/2 cup of water / more, depending on the consistency pinch of black pepper

Toppings:

- Golden berries
- coconut
- bee pollen
- mango

Instructions:

1. Blend all of the ingredients until they are thick and smooth. Add chosen (optional) toppings to the top.

Sweet Potato Toasts

Preparation time: 5 minutes | Total Time: 5 minutes

Servings: 6 | Difficulty Level: Medium

Nutritional Information:

Calories: 151 kcal, Protein: 4.4 g, Carbohydrates: 16.9 g, Fat: 8.4 g, Fiber: 2.5 g

Ingredients:

- 1/4 cup of peanut butter/ almond butter
- 1 medium sweet potato; sliced into 1/4-inch thick slices
- 1 banana; sliced

Instructions:

1. Cut the sweet potato in half and remove the ends. Make 4 slices by slicing them lengthwise into 1/4-inch-thick pieces. Toast the pieces in a toaster. Toast for 2-3 minutes on high or until nicely browned on the outside and cooked through on the inside. Rep with the remaining two slices. Using 1 tablespoon of desired butter, spread 1 tablespoon on each slice. Close the sandwiches by adding banana slices on top.

Southwest Tofu Scramble

Preparation time: 5 minutes | Total time: 30 minutes

Servings: 2 | Difficulty Level: Easy

Nutrition Information:

Calories: 212 Kcal, Protein: 16.4 g, Carbohydrates: 7.1 g, Fat: 15.1 g, Fiber: 3 g

Ingredients

Scramble

- 1-2 Tbsp of avocado oil/olive oil
- 8 ounces of extra-firm tofu
- 1/4 thinly sliced red onion
- 2 cups of loosely chopped kale
- 1/2 thinly sliced red pepper

Sauce

- 1/2 tsp of garlic powder
- 1/2 tsp of sea salt (low quantity for less salty sauce)
- 1/4 tsp of chili powder
- 1/2 tsp of ground cumin
- 1/4 tsp of Turmeric (*optional*)
- Water (too thin)

For Serving (Optional)

- Cilantro
- Salsa
- Breakfast potatoes, fruit, or toast

Instructions

1. Roll tofu in a clean, absorbent cloth for 15 minutes with anything heavy on top, such as a castiron pan. Prepare the sauce by combining dry spices in a small dish and adding enough water to create a pourable sauce while the tofu drains.

Set it aside.

2. Heat a wide skillet on medium heat while preparing the vegetables. When the pan is heated, add the onion, red pepper, and olive oil. Stir in salt and pepper to taste. Cook for 5 minutes or until softened. Add the kale, season with a pinch of salt and pepper, and cover for 2 minutes to steam.
3. Meanwhile, unwrap the tofu and crush it with a fork into bite-sized pieces.
4. Move the vegetables to one side of the pan and add the tofu using a spatula. After 2 minutes, add the sauce and pour it mainly over the tofu and a little over the vegetables. Stir quickly to distribute the sauce evenly. Cook for 5-7 minutes or until the tofu has browned slightly. Serve with toast, breakfast potatoes, or fruit. Spicy sauce, salsa, and fresh cilantro are the favorite ways to ramp up the taste.

Baby Kale Breakfast Salad with Quinoa & Strawberries

Preparation time: 15 minutes | Total time: 15 minutes

Servings: 1 | Difficulty Level: Easy

Nutritional Information:

Calories: 330 Kcal, Protein: 9g, Carbohydrates: 31 g, Fat: 20.1 g, Fiber: 5.9 g

Ingredients:

- 2 teaspoons of apple cider vinegar
- 1 tablespoon of extra-virgin olive oil
- 3 cups of lightly packed baby kale
- 1 teaspoon of minced garlic
- Pinch of ground pepper
- 1/2 cup of cooked quinoa
- 1 tablespoon of salted pepitas
- Pinch of salt
- 1/2 cup of sliced strawberries

Instructions:

1. To make a paste, mash the garlic and salt with a fork or a chef's knife. Mix the oil, garlic paste, vinegar, and pepper in a medium bowl. Stir in the kale and toss to coat. Serve with strawberries, quinoa, and pepitas on the side.

Parsley Frittata

Preparation time: 10 minutes | Total time: 30 minutes

Servings: 4 | Difficulty Level: Medium

Nutritional Information:

Calories: 119 Kcal, Protein: 9.4 g, Carbohydrates: 2.2 g, Fat: 8 g, Fiber: 0.3 g

Ingredients:

- 6 beaten eggs,
- 1/4 cup of plain yogurt
- 1/2 cup of chopped parsley
- 1/2 teaspoon of cayenne pepper
- 1 teaspoon of olive oil

Instructions:

1. Combine parsley, eggs, plain yogurt, and cayenne pepper in a mixing bowl. After that, pour olive oil into the pan and heat it thoroughly. Pour an egg mixture into the skillet, carefully flatten it, and cover it. Cook the frittata for 20 minutes over medium heat.

Oatmeal with Turmeric Powder

Preparation time: 5 minutes | Total time: 20 minutes

Servings: 2 | Difficulty Level: Easy

Nutritional Information:

Calories: 154.6 Kcal, Protein: 5.1 g, Carbohydrates: 29.2 g, Fat: 3.1 g, Fiber: 12 g

Ingredients:

- 1 teaspoon turmeric powder
- 1 cup whole oats, rolled
- 2 milk splashes
- 2 cups water

Instructions:

1. In 2 cups of boiling water, add your oats. Cook for about 10 minutes with the heat reduced to medium, stirring often. About minute five, add your splashes of milk with the teaspoon of turmeric powder, and keep stirring.
2. When the oatmeal is done cooking, spoon it into a bowl and top it with your choice of toppings.
3. You may eat it plain as well. Whatever the case, this oatmeal is both wholesome and tasty.

Zucchini Oatmeal

Preparation time: 10 minutes | Total time: 15 minutes

Servings: 1 | Difficulty Level: Easy

Nutritional Information:

Calories: 226 kcal, Protein: 7 g, Carbohydrates: 34 g, Fat: 9 g, Fiber: 7 g

Ingredients:

- 1 Cup of Zucchini; Shredded
- 1/3 Cup of Oatmeal
- 1 Tbsp of Stevia
- 1 Cup of Unsweetened Almond Milk
- 1/4 Tsp of Nutmeg
- 1 Tsp of Cinnamon
- 1 Tsp of Vanilla Extract
- Dash of Sea Salt
- 1 Tbsp of Pecans; Chopped
- 1 Tbsp of Raisins

Instructions:

1. Boil the milk in a saucepan on the stove, adding all ingredients except the raisins and pecans. Reduce to low heat and cook until most of the liquid has almost been absorbed. Pour into a bowl and top with raisins and pecans when done. Note: You can prepare this up to 4 days ahead of time and keep it in the fridge, then reheat and add toppings when ready to eat.

Appetizer Recipes

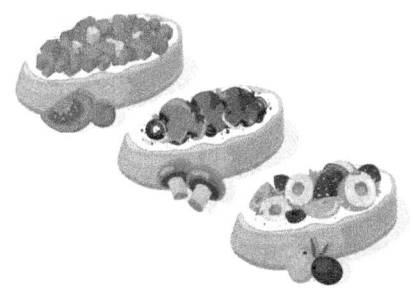

Sweet Potato Soup

Preparation time: 1 hr. | Total time: 1 hr. 10 minutes

Servings: 8 | Difficulty Level: Easy

Nutritional Information:

Calories: 180 Kcal, Protein: 2 g, Carbohydrates: 21 g, Fat: 10 g, Fiber: 4.1 g

Ingredients:

- 1 cubed white onion,
- 4 tablespoons of extra virgin olive oil
- 1 chopped garlic clove, pinch of cinnamon
- 1 teaspoon of black pepper; fresh, cracked
- 3/4 tablespoon of salt
- 1 tablespoon of sweet yellow curry powder pinch of cloves
- 1 teaspoon of cayenne pepper
- 3 medium-sized cubed sweet potatoes
- 1 teaspoon of turmeric
- 4 cups of hot water
- 1 liter of vegetable stock; low-sodium
- 2 medium-sized cubed white potatoes,
- 1 13.66-ounce can of lite coconut milk
- 1 large zucchini; width-wise

Instructions:

1. Clean, chop, and cube all of your veggies. Put it aside. Add 4 tablespoons of extra virgin olive oil to a big saucepan. Add onion and allow it to cook for a few minutes. Allow it to sweat for 5 mins on low heat.
2. Season with pepper, salt, and garlic. Stir it well before adding the potatoes. Add potatoes and allow for a 5-minute cook time on medium heat to get brown color. To prevent burning, keep stirring.

3. Toss in the stalk and a splash of water. Bring to a boil, reduce to low heat, and cook for 20-25 minutes. Add zucchini halfway through the cooking process. Add coconut milk after 20-25 minutes. Do a fork text before putting the soup in the blender to ensure the potatoes are cooked.
4. Purée the soup in a blender. Garnish with lemon juice, black pepper, and herbs and spices.

Broccoli with garlic and lemon

Preparation time: 5 minutes | Total Time: 10 minutes

Servings: 4 | Difficulty Level: Medium

Nutritional Information:

Calories: 45 kcal, Protein: 3 g, carbohydrates: 7 g, Fat: 1 g, Fiber: 3 g

Ingredients:

- 1 teaspoon of olive oil
- 4 cups of broccoli florets
- 1/4 teaspoon of ground black pepper
- 1 tablespoon of minced garlic
- 1/4 teaspoon of kosher salt
- 1 teaspoon of lemon zest

Instructions:

1. Boil one cup of water in a small saucepan. Add broccoli and cook in boiling water for 2 to 3 minutes or until the broccoli is tender. Drain the broccoli and set it aside.
2. Heat the oil in a small sauté pan over medium-high heat. Sauté garlic for 30 seconds. Add salt, lemon zest, broccoli, and pepper. Toss it well and serve it.

Quinoa and Vegetable Soup

Preparation time: 30 minutes | Total time: 1 hr. 15 minutes

Servings:6 | Difficulty Level: Easy

Nutritional Information:

Calories: 280 Kcal, Protein: 11.6 g, Carbohydrates: 31.8 g, Fat: 12.4 g, Fiber: 8.5 g

Ingredients:

- 1 chopped onion
- 2 tablespoons of butter
- 1/2 cup of diced carrot
- 1 minced clove of garlic
- 2 tablespoons of dried parsley
- 1/2 cup of chopped celery
- 1 bay leaf
- 1 teaspoon of dried basil
- 2 tablespoons of olive oil
- 1 pinch of dried thyme
- 2 (32 ounces) cartons of chicken broth
- 2 cups of shredded cabbage
- 1 (28-ounce) can have crushed tomatoes
- 1/2 cup of grated Parmesan cheese
- 1 (15 ounces) can have drained light red kidney beans
- 1/2 cup of quinoa

Instructions:

1. In a wide pot or Dutch oven, heat olive oil and butter over medium heat; sauté and stir the onion, garlic, carrot, and celery until softened, for 5 to 10 minutes.
2. Bring the parsley, basil, thyme, chicken broth, bay leaf, and tomatoes to a boil. Reduce heat to low and cook for 10 minutes or until well heated.

3. Add kidney beans, cabbage, and quinoa. Cover and cook for 30 minutes or until the quinoa is cooked. Serve with a sprinkling of Parmesan cheese on top of each dish.

Beet Hummus

Preparation time: 15 minutes | Total Time: 0 minutes

Servings: 8 | Difficulty Level: Medium

Nutritional Information:

Calories: 224 kcal, Protein: 7 g, Carbohydrates: 20 g, Fat: 14 g, Fiber: 1.8 g

Ingredients:

- 1/3 cup of extra-virgin olive oil
- 4 cups of canned chickpeas; drained and rinsed
- 1 medium beet; cooked, peeled & chopped
- 3 tablespoons of tahini
- 1/4 cup of fresh lemon juice
- 1 garlic clove; smashed
- Pita chips, crackers, tortilla chips, or chopped vegetables, as desired, for dipping
- Kosher salt & freshly ground black pepper

Instructions:

1. Combine the olive oil, chickpeas, beet, tahini, lemon juice and garlic in the bowl of a food processor. Season with salt and pepper after pureeing until smooth. Serve with crackers, chips, and vegetables of your choice.

Asparagus & Snap Pea Salad with Crispy Prosciutto

Preparation time: 5 minutes | Total time: 15 minutes

Servings:4 | Difficulty Level: Easy

Nutritional Information:

Calories: 206 Kcal, Protein: 7 g, Carbohydrates: 13 g, Fat: 14 g, Fiber: 5 g

Ingredients:

- 4 slices of prosciutto
- 1/3 cup of slivered almonds
- 1-pound trimmed asparagus; 2-inch pieces
- 2 tablespoons of olive oil; extra-virgin
- 1/2 teaspoon of fine kosher / sea salt
- 2 tablespoons of balsamic vinegar
- 1/2 pound of snap peas; 1-inch pieces
- 2 tablespoons of minced shallot
- 1 cup of micro radish greens
- 1/4 teaspoon of black pepper; freshly ground

Instructions:

1. Add the asparagus to a large saucepan of salted water and bring it to a boil. Cook for 1-2 minutes or until the asparagus is slightly soft and bright green.
2. Transfer the asparagus to an ice bath using a slotted spoon. Drain when it has cooled.
3. Meanwhile, cook the prosciutto in a wide pan over medium heat. Cook for 5-6 minutes, stirring often until the prosciutto is golden and crispy.
4. Cut prosciutto into tiny pieces after draining on a paper towel-lined dish.
5. In a large mixing bowl, combine the balsamic vinegar, olive

oil, salt, shallot, and pepper. Toss in the snap peas, asparagus, and microgreens until evenly coated.
6. Serve with prosciutto slices and almonds on top.

Tomato & Greens Salad

Preparation time: 5 minutes | Total time: 10 minutes

Servings: 2 | Difficulty Level: Easy

Nutritional Information:

Calories: 90 Kcal, Protein: 1.7 g, Carbohydrates: 6.3 g, Fat: 7.3 g, Fiber: 2.2 g

Ingredients:

- 1/2 tablespoon of fresh lemon juice
- 3 cups of fresh baby greens
- 1 tablespoon of olive oil (extra-virgin)
- 1 -1/2 cups of cherry tomatoes

Instructions:

1. Combine all ingredients in a wide mixing bowl and toss well to combine. Serve it.

Oatmeal Crackers

Preparation time: 10 minutes | Total time: 26 minutes

Servings: 4 | Difficulty Level: Medium

Nutritional Information:

Calories: 135 Kcal, Protein: 3 g, Carbohydrates: 21 g, Fat: 4 g, Fiber: 2 g

Ingredients:

- 1/2 teaspoon of garlic powder
- 5/8 cup of flour blend; gluten-free
- 1 1/2 Tablespoons of melted vegan buttery spread
- 1/4 teaspoon of salt
- 1/2 teaspoon of agave nectar or honey a large flake of sea salt; for sprinkling
- 1/2 cup of old-fashioned oats; gluten-free
- 1/4-1/2 cup of water

Instructions:

1. Preheat the oven to 400 degrees Fahrenheit. In a food processor, grind the gluten-free oats until they form a fine flour. Mix the oat flour, garlic powder, gluten-free flour, and salt in a mixing bowl.
2. Add 1/4 cup of water, agave or honey, buttery spread, and stir it well. More water should be drizzled, stirring until the dough forms a ball. The dough mustn't be overly moist. Put the dough on a parchment paper-lined baking sheet and cover it with waxed paper. Roll out the dough until it is very thin, approximately 1/8 inch thick. Roll the dough out as evenly as you can.
3. Remove the waxed paper and put the dough on the cookie sheet's parchment paper. Use a knife to cut the dough into squares, but do not separate them. Pour a little amount of water over the dough and smooth it up.

4. Top with a sprinkling of sea salt flakes. Bake for 13-16 minutes at 400 degrees, turning the baking sheet once throughout the baking time, until golden brown and crisp. Allow it to cool completely before cutting it into squares.

Grilled Eggplant Provolone

Preparation time: 30 minutes | Total time: 45 minutes

Servings: 8 | Difficulty Level: Medium

Nutritional Information:

Calories: 196 Kcal, Protein: 9 g, Carbohydrates: 13 g, Fat: 13 g, Fiber: 7 g

Ingredients:

- 1/4 teaspoon of dried oregano
- 3 tablespoons of olive oil
- 1/2 teaspoon of kosher salt
- Four small eggplants, half lengthwise
- 1 1/2 tablespoons of balsamic vinegar
- Black pepper; freshly ground
- Grilled Salsa
- 1/2 pound of mild provolone; thick-sliced

Instructions:

1. Brush the sliced sides of the eggplants with a mixture of oil, vinegar, and oregano. Season to taste with pepper and salt. Preheat the gas grill to high; after 15 minutes, reduce the heat to medium. (If using charcoal, cook until the coals are completely coated with grey ash.)
2. Grill eggplants cut-side down for approximately 5 minutes or until browned. Top each half of the eggplant with a piece of provolone. For 3 minutes longer, grill them or until the cheese is bubbling. Serve with a side of Grilled Salsa.

Vegan Kimchi

Preparation time: 20 minutes | Total Time: 0 minutes

Servings: 64 | Difficulty Level: Medium

Nutritional Information:

Calories: 160 kcal, Protein: 6 g, Carbohydrates: 11 g, Fat: 0.5 g, Fiber: 4 g

Ingredients:
- 4 stalks of green onions, only the green part, pieces
- 1 head napa cabbage; (1 lb.)
- 3 tbsp of red pepper flakes
- 4 cloves garlic; minced
- 1/2 cup of onions; thinly sliced
- 1-inch ginger; grated
- 2 tbsp of sea salt
- 1 tsp of sugar

Instructions:
1. Cabbage is cut in 8 wedges vertically. Slices are placed in a big bowl. After 3–4 minutes, add 2 tablespoons of salt and massage it into the cabbage until it is moist and wilts. For 50 minutes, set it aside. Prepare the remaining ingredients in the meantime. Slice 1/2 cup of onions thinly. The green parts of onions are chopped into 2-inch chunks. Garlic cloves are minced. Fresh ginger is grated. Ginger and garlic are combined into a paste by adding 1 tsp sugar. After 50 minutes, put the cabbage into a colander and give it a good one-minute rinse under cold running water. For 30 minutes, drain the cabbage.
2. Add the chopped cabbage, green onion pieces, garlic ginger paste, sliced onions, and 3 tbsp. of red pepper flakes into a large bowl. Mix well until combined. Fill clean jars with the mixture, leaving 1 inch of space at the top for fermentation.

Place in the refrigerator for up to months for storage after three days on the counter at room temperature. In the refrigerator, fermentation will continue to occur. After three days, the kimchi's top may seem frothy or include tiny bubbles, which indicates fermentation. Kimchi should be thrown out if it smells bad or appears slimy.

Mixed Fruit Salad

Preparation time: 5 minutes | Total Time: 10 minutes

Servings: 2 | Difficulty Level: Medium

Nutritional Information:

Calories: 79.2 kcal, Protein: 1.2 g, Carbohydrates: 31.8 g, Fat: 0.5 g, Fiber: 4.5 g

Ingredients:

- 1 Kiwi Fruit
- 1/2 cup small Apples (approx. 4 per lb.)
- 1/2 cup of Raspberries
- 1/2 medium Bananas

Instructions:

1. Combine bananas, apples, raspberries, and kiwi in a bowl and serve it.

Grilled Tomatoes

Preparation time: 5 minutes | Total Time: 15 minutes

Servings: 2-4 | Difficulty Level: Medium

Nutritional Information:

Calories: 43 kcal, Protein: 1 g, Carbohydrates: 6 g, Fat: 2 g, Fiber: 2 g

Ingredients:

- 2 ripe tomatoes, halved vertically
- Olive oil
- Kosher salt

Instructions:

1. Cut fresh tomatoes vertically in half, rub them with a little salt and olive oil, and then grill them.

Beet Salad

Preparation time: 10 minutes | Total Time: 55 minutes

Servings: 4 | Difficulty Level: Easy

Nutritional Information:

Calories: 283 kcal, Protein: 6 g, Carbohydrates: 16 g, Fat: 16 g, Fiber: 3.8 g

Ingredients:

- 2-3 ounces of Stilton or blue cheese
- 4, beets (peeled, roasted, chilled, and diced)
- 1/4 cup of fresh basil chopped fine.
- 1/2 cup of pecans or walnuts
- 1/2 cup of fruit or herb vinegar
- Lettuce leaf :1 per person
- 2 tablespoons of olive oil

Instructions:

1. Heat the oven to 400°F. Bake beets until soft for 45 mins and cool, peel, and slice them. In a saucepan, add the sugar, water, and nuts. Heat the mixture, stirring continuously until most liquid bubbles are absorbed. Place nuts on aluminum foil until coated and the frying pan is dry. Let it cool, and it can be kept for many months at room temperature. Put up a lettuce bed. Toss the vinegar, basil, and oil with the beets. Spread it on a lettuce bed. Sprinkle nuts and cheese cubes over it. Serve.

Winter Orange & Fennel Salad

Preparation time: 10 minutes | Total Time: 10 minutes

Servings: 4 | Difficulty Level: Easy

Nutritional Information:

Calories: 198 kcal, Protein: 4 g, Carbohydrates: 30 g, Fat: 9 g, Fiber: 7 g

Ingredients:

- 1 large Sicilian orange
- 1/2 bulb fennel fine sea salt
- Black pepper, freshly cracked
- fresh Sicilian olive oil

Instructions:

1. Peel the fennel into wedges. Slice an orange horizontally after removing all skin, including the white, using a sharp knife. Slice the fennel very thin. Combine in a bowl with fresh olive oil, pepper, and a dash of fine sea salt.

Parsley Sauce

Preparation time: 10 minutes | Total Time: 5 minutes

Servings: 4 | Difficulty Level: Easy

Nutritional Information:

Calories: 103 kcal, Protein: 3 g, Carbohydrates: 7 g, Fat: 7 g, Fiber: 1 g

Ingredients:

- 1/4 cup of Ligurian olive oil
- 1 clove of garlic bunch of parsley
- 1 lemon zest
- Salt and pepper; to taste
- 1 small hot pepper

Instructions:

1. Blend all ingredients in the processor and enjoy.

☆ ☆ ☆ ☆ ☆

Celery Root Salad

Preparation time: 10 minutes | Total time: 5 minutes

Servings:4 | Difficulty Level: Easy

Nutritional Information:

Calories: 66 kcal, protein: 2.3 g, carbohydrates: 14.4 g, Fat: 0.5 g, Fiber: 2.8 g

Ingredients:

- parsley
- 1/2 head of red cabbage; sliced horizontally
- 1 lemon juiced
- 1/2 celery root; sliced thin salt & paprika; to taste

Instructions:

1. Mix all ingredients in a medium bowl, stir, and serve

☆ ☆ ☆ ☆ ☆

Meat Recipes

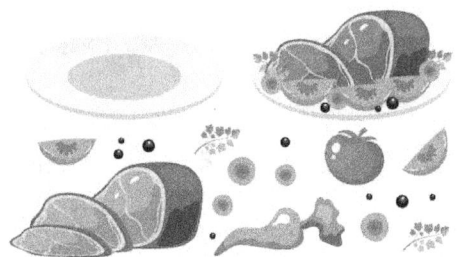

Chicken, Avocado & Quinoa Bowls with Herb Dressing

Preparation time: 15 minutes | Total time: 30 minutes

Servings: 4 | Difficulty Level: Medium

Nutritional Information:

Calories: 753 Kcal, Protein: 34.4 g, Carbohydrates: 43.3 g, Fat: 50 g, Fiber: 10.3 g

Ingredients:

- 5 skinless, boneless chicken thighs (1 1/4 pounds); trimmed
- Roasted Chicken Thighs
- 1/4 teaspoon of salt
- 1/2 teaspoon of ground pepper

Quinoa

- 1 tablespoon of olive oil; extra-virgin
- 3 cups of chicken broth; low-sodium
- 1 1/2 cups of quinoa
- 1/4 teaspoon of salt

Italian Dressing

- 5 tablespoons of water
- 3/4 cup of red wine vinegar
- 2 teaspoons of dried oregano
- 1 large clove of garlic
- 2 teaspoons of dried basil
- 1 1/2 tablespoons of sugar
- 1/2 teaspoon of salt
- 1 tablespoon of Dijon mustard
- 1 3/4 cups of olive oil; extra-virgin
- 1/2 teaspoon of ground pepper

Toppings

- 1 sliced avocado,
- 1 (15-ounce) can of chickpeas; rinsed
- 6 thinly sliced radishes,
- 1/4 cup of toasted seeds/chopped nuts
- 1 cup of sprouts or shoots

Instructions:

1. Preheat the oven to 425 degrees Fahrenheit. Place the chicken on the baking pan. Sprinkle 1/4 teaspoon of salt and 1/2 teaspoon of ground pepper to taste. Roast the chicken for 14 to 16 minutes or until the instant-read thermometer in the thickest portion registers 165 degrees F. Cut 4 thighs.
2. In a large pot, combine 1 tablespoon of oil, broth, and 1/4 teaspoon salt. Bring to a boil over high heat, then reduce to low heat and stir in the quinoa. Reduce heat to low and cook for 15 to 20 minutes until the quinoa has absorbed all liquid and the grains have burst. Take the pan off the heat, cover it, and set it aside for 5 minutes. (Set aside 2 cups for later.)
3. To make the dressing in a blender, combine the water, vinegar, sugar, mustard, basil, garlic, salt, oregano, and pepper. Puree until completely smooth. Slowly drizzle in the oil and purée until the mixture is creamy. (Refrigerate 1 3/4 cups in a big mason jar for up to one week.)
4. To make the bowls: Distribute 3 cups of quinoa into 4 big shallow dishes. Put chickpeas, radishes, chicken, avocado, and sprouts in it. Sprinkle seeds on it. Drizzle 3/4 cup of dressing on top.

White Bean and Chicken Chili Blanca

Preparation time: 15 minutes | Total time: 1 hr. 20 minutes

Servings: 8 | Difficulty Level: Medium

Nutritional Information:

Calories: 180.3 Kcal, Protein: 15 g, Carbohydrates: 16 g, Fat: 6 g, Fiber: 1 g

Ingredients:

- 2 tablespoons of olive oil; extra-virgin
- 1 pound of chicken tenders / skinless, boneless chicken breasts
- 2 garlic cloves
- 1 medium diced onion
- 2 tablespoons of chopped fresh cilantro
- 1 cup of corn kernels, fresh or frozen, thawed
- 2 15-ounce cans of white beans; drained and rinsed
- 2 teaspoons of ground cumin
- 2 cups of Monterey Jack cheese, grated
- 1 4-ounce can of chopped green chiles
- 2 teaspoons of pure chili powder
- 3 cups of water
- 1/8 teaspoon of cayenne pepper

Instructions:

1. Using salt and pepper, season the chicken. Heat oil in a large skillet over high heat, add the chicken pieces, cook it, and occasionally turn until browned; it will take about 2-3 minutes. Reduce the heat to medium-low and add the onion and garlic. Cook for 5-6 minutes or until the onion is transparent. Add chiles, beans, spices, corn, and water. Bring to a boil, lower to low heat, and let simmer for 1 hour, uncovered. Add a tablespoon of cheese and a sprinkle of cilantro to each serving.

☆ ☆ ☆ ☆ ☆

Roasted Chicken With Balsamic Vinaigrette

Preparation time: 15 minutes | Total time: 1 hr. (plus 2 to 24 hours for chicken to marinate) | Servings:4 | Difficulty Level: Medium

Nutritional Information:

Calories: 189.9 Kcal, Protein: 24.4 g, Carbohydrates: 8.1 g, Fat: 7.3 g, Fiber: 2 g

Ingredients:
- 2 tablespoons of Dijon mustard
- 1 teaspoon of lemon zest
- 2 tablespoons of fresh lemon juice
- 1/4 cup of balsamic vinegar
- 2 chopped garlic cloves
- Salt
- 2 tablespoons of olive oil
- 1 (4-pound) whole chicken; sliced
- black pepper; freshly ground
- 1/2 cup of chicken broth; low-salt
- 1 tablespoon of fresh parsley leaves; chopped

Instructions:

1. Whisk together the mustard, lemon juice, vinegar, olive oil, salt, garlic, and pepper in a small bowl. In a wide resealable plastic bag, combine the chicken pieces and vinaigrette; close the bag and toss them to coat. Refrigerate for about 2 hours and up to one day, rotating the chicken pieces periodically.
2. Preheat oven to 400 degrees Fahrenheit. Remove the chicken from the bag and place it in a large baking dish that has been sprayed. Roast for 1 hour or until chicken is cooked through. Cover the chicken with foil for the cooking time if it browns too fast. Place the chicken on a serving dish and serve.

3. Place the baking dish on a low-medium heat stove. Scrape up any browned pieces on the bottom of a baking sheet with a wooden spoon and whisk them into the broth and pan drippings. Drizzle the chicken with the pan drippings. Serve the chicken with parsley and lemon zest.

Sweet & Sour Chicken

Preparation time: 15 minutes | Total time: 30 minutes

Servings: 3 | Difficulty Level: Easy

Nutritional Information:

Calories: 290.6 Kcal, Protein: 8 g, Carbohydrates: 52 g, Fat: 5 g, Fiber: 1 g

Ingredients:

- 1 tbsp of tomato puree
- 1/2 cube of chicken stock
- 6 tbsp of apple juice /pineapple juice
- 1 tbsp of rice wine /sherry
- 1 tsp of coconut oil/vegetable oil
- 1 tbsp of rice vinegar /white wine vinegar
- 1 tbsp of corn flour
- 1 clove of garlic
- 400 g chicken breast
- 1 tsp of fresh ginger; grated
- 1 whole green pepper
- 1 spring onion
- 1 whole red pepper
- 150 g fresh pineapple/ 2 rings of tinned pineapple
- 1 medium onion

Instructions:

1. For sauce making, combine 1/2 stock cube with the 2 tbsp of boiling water in a heat-proof dish and stir until dissolved. Add vinegar, apple/pineapple juice, rice wine, tomato puree, and corn flour. Stir well and set aside. Cut onions, peppers, and pineapple into 2 cm pieces and set aside. Reserve the chicken breast, which should be chopped into the same size cubes as the veggies. Garlic and ginger should be coarsely grated or

2. crushed, and spring onions should be neatly sliced. Heat the oil in a wok or heavy-bottomed pan over high heat.
3. Add ginger, garlic, and spring onion, then the chicken. Stir-fry chicken for 5-6 mins over high
4. heat, stirring continuously, until it is fully done. If necessary, add a tbsp. of water at a time. Stir in the onions and peppers for a further 2 minutes. Remove from heat and whisk in the pineapple and sauce until the sauce has thickened and is boiling. Serve with rice or gluten-free noodles.

Pulled Pork

Preparation time: 10 minutes | Total time: 8-10 hours slow cooker cooking | Servings:4 | Difficulty Level: Medium

Nutritional Information:

Calories: 254 Kcal, Protein: 15 g, Carbohydrates: 16 g, Fat: 14 g, Fiber: 2 g

Ingredients:

- 2 teaspoons of sumac
- 1 tablespoon of dark brown sugar
- 2kg pork shoulder (joint or steaks)
- 3 tablespoons of apple cider vinegar
- 2 teaspoons of garlic salt
- 2 tablespoons of black treacle or molasses
- 150 ml apple juice

To serve

- Slices of fresh apple
- Gluten freerolls Apple sauce
- white and red cabbage; Shredded

Instructions:

1. Sumac, garlic salt/salt, and dark brown sugar are rubbed into the pork. Place it in a slow cooker or a big saucepan with a cover. Pour the vinegar, apple juice, and treacle/molasses over the meat. Cover and cook on Low for 8-10 hours in a slow cooker or 2 hours per kilogram in a normal oven at 140C/120 Fan. Shoulder steaks cook faster than joint steaks. Take the pork out of the fluids after it has finished cooking. Using two forks, shred the meat. To remove the fat, strain the liquid and chill it. Reheat the pork with the drained liquids before serving it with your favorite toppings on a bun.

☆ ☆ ☆ ☆ ☆

Turkey Shepherd's Pie

Preparation time: 15 minutes | Total time: 35 minutes

Servings:6 | Difficulty Level: Medium

Nutritional Information:

Calories: 384 Kcal, Protein: 35 g, Carbohydrates: 34 g, Fat: 12 g, Fiber: 6 g

Ingredients:

- 2 teaspoons of olive oil
- 1.5 pounds of ground turkey
- 3 Tablespoons of ketchup
- 1 chopped onion
- 1 cup of white button-sliced mushrooms
- 2 minced cloves of garlic
- 1 cup of frozen peas
- 3/4 cup of non-dairy milk
- 1/8 teaspoon of white pepper
- 3 Tablespoons of buttery vegan spread
- 6 peeled gold potatoes; large chunks
- 1/2 teaspoon of salt
- 3/4 cup of cheddar cheese; non-dairy
- 1/2 cup of non-dairy milk

Instructions:

Turn the broiler into a large skillet, and heat olive oil over medium heat. Add mushrooms, garlic, chopped onion, and turkey. Cook until the turkey is fully done. The grease should be removed. Boil the potatoes in a separate pan for approximately 20 minutes while the turkey is cooking. Drain the water, add salt, vegan butter, and ½ cup of milk, and mash the potato with a potato masher.

Toss the ground turkey with pepper, ketchup, and 3/4 cup of non-dairy milk. Stir constantly over low heat until the sauce has thickened somewhat. Stir in the peas until they are well cooked.

Fill a casserole dish halfway with the turkey mixture. Distribute evenly. Spread the mashed potatoes over the turkey and spread them out evenly. Cheese is sprinkled on top. Cover the casserole dish with foil and broil for 5 minutes or until the cheese is browned and melted.

Cheesy Broccoli Chicken Rice

Preparation time: 10 minutes | Total time: 4 hours 10 minutes

Servings:8 | Difficulty Level: Medium

Nutritional Information:

Calories: 272 Kcal, Protein: 21 g, Carbohydrates: 26 g, Fat: 8 g, Fiber: 2 g

Ingredients:

- 1 chopped onion
- 1 1/2 pounds of chicken breasts; large chunks
- 1 coarsely chopped clove of garlic
- 32 ounces of chicken broth
- 1 cup of long-grain rice; brown or white; uncooked
- 1/3 teaspoon of pepper
- 1 1/4 teaspoons of salt
- 1 Tablespoon of olive oil
- 1 1/4 cups of cheddar cheese; dairy-free
- 2 cups of broccoli, chopped

Instructions:

1. Add diced onion, olive oil, and garlic to the slow cooker's bottom. Then add salt, chicken breasts, and pepper, as well as the rice. Add 2/3 of the broth container. Stir. Turn the slow cooker on high and cover it. Cook on high for four hours. Check to see whether there is enough liquid inside after two hours. If necessary, add additional warmed broth. Stir in the chopped broccoli half an hour before it's done. If necessary, add additional heated broth. Cook for another 30 minutes until the broccoli is green and soft. Stir in the cheese until it melts. If desired, season with additional salt and pepper. Serve right away.

Seafood Recipes

Blackened Salmon

Preparation time: 10 minutes | Total time: 20 minutes

Servings: 4 | Difficulty Level: Medium

Nutritional Information:

Calories: 485 Kcal, Protein: 46 g, Carbohydrates: 30 g, Fat: 19 g, Fiber: 3 g

Ingredients:

- 1 Tablespoon of olive oil or butter
- 4 6 oz salmon fillets; skin-on
- 3 Tablespoons of blackened seasoning /Cajun seasoning
- 2 cups of white, brown /cauliflower rice; for serving
- Pineapple salsa; for serving

Instructions

1. If necessary, make a blackened seasoning. Apply a generous amount of blackened seasoning to each salmon fillet's meat. Heat the oil or butter in a wide nonstick /cast iron pan over medium heat. Cook the fillets, skin-side up, in the pan until browned, for approximately 3 minutes. Cook, flipping once or twice until the fillets are cooked to your liking, for around 5 to 7 minutes, depending on the thickness of the fillets. Serve over rice with pineapple salsa on top.

Garlic Shrimp and Asparagus with Zucchini Noodles

Preparation time:10 minutes | Total time: 20 minutes

Servings:2 | Difficulty Level: Medium

Nutritional Information:

Calories: 321 Kcal, Protein: 37 g, Carbohydrates: 23 g, Fat: 9 g, Fiber: 8 g

Ingredients:

- 1 lb. asparagus; trimmed and chopped
- 1 Tablespoon of olive oil
- 1/2 teaspoon of sea salt
- 5 minced garlic cloves
- 1/4-1 teaspoon of crushed red pepper
- 1 lb. peeled and deveined shrimp
- 1/4 teaspoon of black pepper; freshly ground
- 2 Tablespoons of fresh lemon juice parsley for garnish; fresh chopped
- 2 medium zucchinis; spiralized into noodles

Instructions

1. In a wide nonstick skillet, heat the oil over medium heat. Add salt, asparagus, red pepper, garlic, and black pepper, and cook for 2 minutes. Cook, often stirring, for approximately 4 minutes after adding the shrimp. Add the lemon juice and mix well. Transfer the mixture to a dish and put it aside after the shrimp is cooked.
2. Sauté zucchini noodles in the same skillet for 1-2 minutes before returning the shrimp and asparagus combination to the pan. Stir to incorporate everything, remove it from the heat, and serve with fresh parsley.

☆☆☆☆☆

Superfood Baked Salmon

Preparation time:5 minutes | Total time: 20 minutes

Servings:4 | Difficulty Level: Medium

Nutritional Information:

Calories: 395Kcal, Protein: 23.7 g, Carbohydrates: 12.4 g, Fat: 28.1 g, Fiber: 2.8 g

Ingredients:

- 2 cups of brussels sprouts (quartered)
- 3 to 4 salmon fillets; (4–5 ounces each)
- 1/4 to 1/3 olive oil
- 1/4 to 1/3 cup of chopped fresh basil
- 1 cup of fresh blueberries
- 3 tbsp of balsamic vinegar
- 1/4 to 1/2 tsp of crushed black Pepper
- 2 cloves / 1 tsp of minced Garlic
- 2 Lemons; one juiced & one sliced
- Sea Salt

Instructions

1. Preheat the oven to 400 degrees Fahrenheit. Clean salmon fillets and put them on a parchmentlined baking sheet. Brussels sprouts should be cleaned and chopped. Place them in the pan. Season the salmon and vegetables with a generous amount of sea salt. Set it aside. Put blueberries in a bowl. Using a fork, mash a little. Add 1/4 teaspoon of salt, basil, 1/4 cup of extra virgin olive oil, 1/4 teaspoon of pepper, garlic, and balsamic vinegar. Combine all of the ingredients. Drizzle 2 to 3 tablespoons of extra virgin olive oil over the fish and Brussels sprouts. Over the salmon fillets, spoon the balsamic basil blueberry mixture.
2. Fresh lemon juice should be squeezed over the fish and

vegetables. On the sheet pan, place lemon slices on top of the vegetables. Add black pepper if desired, and bake for 15 minutes. Broil for 1 to 2 minutes to crisp up the baked salmon skin and Brussels sprouts. Remove the dish from the oven. Serve and have fun!

Roasted Salmon, Smoky Chickpeas, and Greens

Preparation time: 30 minutes | Total time: 40 minutes

Servings:4 | Difficulty Level: Medium

Nutritional Information:

Calories: 447 Kcal, Protein: 37 g, Carbohydrates: 23.4 g, Fat: 21.8 g, Fiber: 6.4 g

Ingredients:

- 1 tablespoon of smoked paprika
- 2 tablespoons of olive oil; extra-virgin, divided
- 1 can (15 ounces) of chickpeas; salt-free, rinsed
- 1/2 teaspoon of salt; divided and a pinch
- 1/4 cup of fresh chopped chives/dill, and more for garnish
- 1/3 cup of buttermilk
- 1/4 cup of mayonnaise
- 1/4 teaspoon of garlic powder
- 1/2 teaspoon of ground pepper, divided
- 10 cups of chopped kale
- 1 1/4 pound of wild salmon; 4 portions
- 1/4 cup of water

Instructions

1. Preheat an oven to 425 degrees F, with racks in the top third and center. Mix paprika, 1 tablespoon of oil, and 1/4 teaspoon salt in a medium mixing dish. Toss the chickpeas with the paprika mixture after completely drying them. Spread the mixture on the rimmed baking sheet. Bake the chickpeas for 30 minutes on the top rack, stirring twice.
2. Meanwhile, mix the mayonnaise in a blender, 1/4 teaspoon of pepper, buttermilk, herbs, and garlic powder until smooth. Put it aside. In a large pan, heat the remaining 1 tablespoon of oil

over medium heat. Cook, stirring periodically, for 2 minutes after adding the greens. Add and cook kale, occasionally stirring, until soft, for approximately 5 minutes longer. Remove the pan from the heat and add a pinch of salt.
3. Take the chickpeas out of the oven and place them on one side of the pan. Put salmon on another side of the pan and season the salmon with the remaining 1/4 tsp of salt and pepper. Bake for 5 to 8 minutes or until the salmon is cooked through. Serve the salmon with the greens and chickpeas, drizzling the leftover dressing on top and garnishing with additional herbs if preferred.

Sheet Pan Turmeric Salmon With Cherry Sauce

Preparation time: 10 minutes | Total time: 25 minutes

Servings:4 | Difficulty Level: Medium

Nutritional Information:

Calories: 304 Kcal, Protein: 32 g, Carbohydrates: 8 g, Fat: 16 g, Fiber: 2 g

Ingredients:

- 1/2 teaspoon of cinnamon
- 1-pound wild salmon
- 1/2 teaspoon of kosher salt
- 1 teaspoon of turmeric
- 1 bunch of broccolis rabe; washed & ends trimmed
- 1/4 teaspoon of garlic powder
- 1-2 tablespoons of olive oil; extra virgin
- 1/4 teaspoon of black pepper; freshly ground

For The Cherry Sauce:

- 1 minced cloves garlic
- 1 1/2 cups of frozen cherries
- 1 tablespoon of water
- 1/2 tablespoon of lemon juice
- 1/2 teaspoon of arrowroot powder
- salt and pepper; to taste

Instructions

1. Preheat the oven to 425 degrees Fahrenheit. In a small dish, combine the spices. Place the salmon on a large baking sheet and rub the spice mixture over it. Surround the fish with broccoli rabe. Drizzle olive oil and leftover spice combination over the broccoli. Place it in the oven for 10-15 mins, or until

salmon is cooked and broccoli rabe begins to wilt to your taste.

For the cherry sauce

2. Add garlic, frozen cherries, pepper, salt, and lemon juice in a small saucepan over medium heat. Once the cherries are cooking, use a spatula to split them up. Cook until most of the water has evaporated. In a small dish, combine the water and arrowroot powder. Reduce heat, add to the cherry mixture, and whisk for 30 sec before removing from the heat. Serve on top of fish that has been cooked.

Creamy Sundried Tomato Pan Seared Sole

Preparation time: 5 minutes | Total time: 20 minutes

Servings: 2 | Difficulty Level: Medium

Nutritional Information:

Calories: 300 Kcal, Protein: 14 g, Carbohydrates: 47 g, Fat: 6 g, Fiber: 7 g

Ingredients:

- 2 tbsp. of olive oil; extra virgin
- 1 tsp. of dried thyme
- 2 sole fillets
- 1/2 cup of vegetable broth
- 2 tbsp. of minced garlic
- salt & pepper; to taste
- 1/4 cup of sundried tomatoes

Instructions

1. In a large pan, warm extra virgin olive oil over medium heat. Add broth, minced garlic, and sundried tomatoes. Cook for another 2-3 minutes, and add salt, sole fillets, and pepper. Add and cook fillets for 3 minutes. Cook for another 3 minutes with the lid on the pan. Reduce the heat to low and add the dried thyme.

Fish Ceviche

Preparation time: 25 minutes | Total time: 30 minutes

Servings: 2 | Difficulty Level: Medium

Nutritional Information:

Calories: 82 Kcal, Protein: 15 g, Carbohydrates: 2.6 g, Fat: 1.3 g, Fiber: 0.5 g

Ingredients:

- 1 cucumber
- 1/2 small red onion
- 1 small mango
- 2 lbs. haddock/ codfish
- 1 tbsp of sea salt
- 9 limes
- 1 1/2 tbsp of pink peppercorn
- 1/2 bunch of cilantro
- 1 small slice of watermelon
- 2 serrano peppers
- 1 tbsp of EVOO

Instructions

1. Cut fish into approximately 1/2-inch-long pieces and blanch it for 3 minutes in boiling water, take it out, and cool it on ice. Put the fish in a bowl. Add 1 tbsp of EVOO and the juice of 5 limes. Allow 10 minutes to marinate in the refrigerator. Meanwhile, combine the pink peppercorn, sea salt, coarsely chopped serrano pepper, cilantro, and cucumber in a mortar and pestle. One lime should be squeezed, and everything should be ground until it resembles an Italian pesto (or use a food processor or blender).
2. Put the remaining diced cucumber (with skin on) in a dish and cubed mango. Squeeze the remaining limes and add red onion

and finely chopped cilantro. Toss together all of the ingredients. Add avocado and marinated fish (and watermelon if using). Mix everything with care. For 5 minutes in the refrigerator, chill it before serving.

Thai Green Curry with Shrimp and Kale

Preparation time: 15 minutes | Total time: 25 minutes

Servings: 4 | Difficulty Level: Medium

Nutritional Information:

Calories: 398 Kcal, Protein: 20 g, Carbohydrates: 60 g, Fat: 9.7 g, Fiber: 4 g

Ingredients:

- 1 tablespoon of chopped fresh garlic
- 2 teaspoons of olive oil
- 1 tablespoon of chopped fresh ginger
- 1/3 cup of chopped green onions
- 1 1/4 cups of matchstick-cut carrots
- 2 tablespoons of Thai green curry paste
- 1 (13.5-ounce) can of light coconut milk
- 1/2 cup of unsalted chicken stock
- 6 cups of packed Lacinato kale; chopped (about 1/2 bunch)
- 1 pound of medium shrimp; peeled and deveined
- 1/4 teaspoon of kosher salt
- 6 ounces of dried rice noodles
- 1/4 cup of chopped fresh cilantro
- 1 1/2 teaspoons of fresh lime juice
- 1 teaspoon of grated lime rind

Instructions

Prepare rice noodles as directed on the box. Rinse them with cold water after draining; drain them and put them aside. In a wide skillet, heat the oil over medium-high heat. Sauté garlic, green onions, and ginger for 1 minute. Stir in the curry paste and cook for another 30 seconds. Add chicken stock, carrots, and coconut milk; bring to a boil, and cook for 5 minutes.

Add kale and season with salt. Cook for 3 minutes or until the kale is soft and wilted. Add and cook shrimp for 3 minutes or until cooked through. Remove from the heat and serve with lime rind, cilantro, and juice on top. Serve with rice noodles on the side.

Vegetable Recipes

Vegan Roasted Pumpkin Curry

Preparation time: 15 minutes | Total time: 45 minutes

Servings: 4 | Difficulty Level: Medium

Nutritional Information:

Calories: 110 Kcal, Protein: 1.9 g, Carbohydrates: 9.1 g, Fat: 7.5 g, Fiber: 2.5 g

Ingredients:

Curry

- 1 onion
- 2 Tbsp of coconut oil (grape seed oil)
- 2 Tbsp of fresh ginger minced
- 1 pumpkin/butternut squash; peeled and cubed
- 2 Tbsp of garlic minced.
- 1 can of coconut milk; full fat
- 2 Tbsp of a curry spice blend
- 1 tsp of salt
- 200 g firm tofu
- 2 Tbsp of lemon juice

Serve

- 2/3 cup of roasted cashews coconut
- yogurt
- flatbread
- chopped parsley

Instructions:

1. To begin, preheat the oven to 220 degrees Celsius. Scrape and cube the pumpkin, then place it on a baking pan with a little oil coating. Bake for at least 20 minutes or until tender. In the meanwhile, warm a wide saucepan over medium-high heat. Add the onion, coconut oil, and ginger once the pan is heated.

Cook, stirring regularly, for 2-3 minutes. Cook for an additional 2 minutes after adding the curry spice mix.
2. After that, add garlic and continue to sauté for a minute. Then, over medium heat, add coconut milk and bring to a simmer. Reduce heat and cover after it has reached a simmering point. Cook, stirring periodically, for 5 minutes.
3. Check the pumpkin at this point; if it's soft, put it in a blender and puree it with a little water until smooth. Add this puree with coconut milk to the pan and season with lemon juice and salt to taste.
4. Set aside and cook cubed tofu in 3 tbsp coconut oil until it develops a lovely golden crust. Serve with rice, flatbread, quinoa, or buckwheat as a side dish. Adding cashews, coconut yogurt, and parsley to the serving dish elevates the meal. Fresh is best, but leftovers may be kept in the refrigerator for up to 3 days.

Ratatouille

Preparation time: 55 minutes | Total time: 1hr. 10 minutes

Servings:4 | Difficulty Level: Easy

Nutritional Information:

Calories: 283 kcal, Protein: 6 g, Carbohydrates: 30 g, Fat: 18 g, Fiber: 4 g

Ingredients:

- 2 sprigs of oregano
- 2 smashed garlic cloves
- 5 tablespoons of olive oil
- 2 medium thickly sliced summer squash
- 1 small thickly sliced eggplant
- 2 medium thickly sliced zucchini
- 1 cup of tomato puree (or tomato sauce)
- 2 small halved red bell peppers; sides cut off
- 1 medium thickly sliced red onion
- 3 medium thickly sliced tomatoes
- Salt and black pepper; freshly ground
- 2 tablespoons of thyme leaves

Instructions:

1. Preheat the oven to 375 degrees Fahrenheit. Place four pans or 1 9-inch square baking dish on a baking sheet. Heat olive oil and garlic in a small saucepan over medium-low heat. Cook for 1 minute or until aromatic. Remove the saucepan from the heat, add oregano, and cook it for 15 minutes. Garlic and oregano should be removed and discarded. Add 2 teaspoons of olive oil to the bottom of each baking dish. Add 2 tablespoons of tomato puree to the bottom of each baking dish. Layer the onion, eggplant, summer squash, pepper, zucchini, and tomato in the prepared baking pan. Don't worry

about flawless or matching the slices; make sure they're all packed in firmly. Drizzle the remaining oil equally over the top, then brush the remaining tomato puree. Season with salt & pepper and a sprig of thyme. Roast for 25 to 30 minutes until soft and brown on the top and edges. Allow 5 to 10 minutes to cool before serving.

Carrot Ginger Soup

Preparation time: 10 minutes | Total time: 40 minutes

Servings: 6 | Difficulty Level: Easy

Nutritional Information:

Calories: 210 kcal, Protein: 5 g, Carbohydrates: 29 g, Fat: 9 g, Fiber: 7 g

Ingredients:

- 2 pounds peeled and chopped carrots
- 1 medium diced yellow onion
- 3 minced cloves of garlic
- 1 tablespoon of grated fresh ginger
- 1/2 teaspoon of turmeric
- 1 (15-oz) can of full-fat coconut milk; divided
- 1 teaspoon of ground cumin
- 1 1/2 teaspoons of salt; to taste
- Pinch of cayenne pepper; optional
- 32 ounces of vegetable broth; low sodium

Instructions:

1. Add 1/2 cup of coconut milk, carrots, onion, grated ginger, cumin, garlic, and turmeric, in a large saucepan, and sauté over medium heat until carrots soften and everything is aromatic approximately 8 minutes. You can speed up the process by covering the pot and stirring occasionally.
2. Add vegetable broth and remaining coconut milk. Raise the heat to high and bring the mixture to a full boil. Reduce to low heat and cover, and cook for about 20 to 30 minutes or until carrots are tender.
3. Transfer everything to a blender and mix until smooth (this may need to be done in stages). Let the steam escape by gently opening the steam vent at the top of the lid, then mix at

medium speed.
4. Unless the soup is already at the appropriate temperature, return the smooth carrot soup to the saucepan and cook for a few minutes. If you must reheat the soup on the stove, do it carefully; else, your tasty soup will turn into a cauldron of boiling, spurting lava.
5. Serve with a dollop of coconut milk yogurt, fresh cilantro, sesame seeds, and a drizzle of coconut milk.

Curry Tofu

Preparation time: 20 minutes | Total time: 25 minutes

Servings:4 | Difficulty Level: Easy

Nutritional Information:

Calories: 180 kcal, Protein: 10.1 g, Carbohydrates: 4 g, Fat: 15.5 g, Fiber: 1.9 g

Ingredients:

- 1 tablespoon of olive oil
- 1 teaspoon of curry powder
- 1-pound cubed tofu,
- 1 teaspoon of grated lemon zest
- 1/2 cup of coconut cream

Instructions:

1. Combine curry powder, coconut cream, olive oil, and lemon zest in a mixing bowl. Then add the tofu and thoroughly combine. Allow 10 minutes for the mixture to marinade. The skillet should be properly preheated. Cook the tofu for 2 minutes on each side.

Cumin Zucchini Rings

Preparation time: 25 minutes | Total time: 15 minutes

Servings:4 | Difficulty Level: Easy

Nutritional Information:

Calories: 48 kcal, Protein: 1.6 g, Carbohydrates: 4.5 g, Fat: 3.3 g, Fiber: 1.4 g

Ingredients:

- 1 tablespoon of cumin seeds
- 3 sliced zucchinis,
- 1/4 teaspoon of cayenne pepper
- 1 tablespoon of olive oil

Instructions:

1. The baking paper should be used to line the baking pan. Arrange zucchini slices in a single layer on the baking pan. Olive oil, cumin seeds, and cayenne pepper are then sprinkled on top and baked at 360°F for 15 minutes.

Instant Pot Potato Leek Soup

Preparation time: 20 minutes | Total time: 26 minutes

Servings:5 | Difficulty Level: Easy

Nutritional Information:

Calories: 364 kcal, Protein: 9 g, Carbohydrates: 44 g, Fat: 13 g, Fiber: 4 g

Ingredients:

- 1 small diced onion
- 2 tablespoons of grapeseed oil
- 3-4 minced cloves of garlic
- 3 medium cleaned & sliced leeks; (white and light green parts)
- 1/2 teaspoon of dried rosemary
- 3/4 teaspoon of dried thyme
- 5 small peeled and chopped russet potatoes (2 pounds)
- 1/2 teaspoon of ground coriander
- 4 cups of vegetable broth; low sodium
- 1 teaspoon of salt; more to taste
- 2 bay leaves
- 1 cup of canned coconut milk
- Fresh ground pepper; to taste

Instructions:

1. Add the oil to Instant Pot and turn ON the sauté command. Add the onions and leeks once the oil is hot. Sauté for 4-6 minutes or until softened. Add rosemary, garlic, thyme, and coriander. Sauté for 30-60 seconds or until aromatic.
2. Turn OFF the sauté function. Add vegetable broth, potatoes, salt, bay leaf, and pepper. Close the lid and fasten it. The steam release handle should be in the Sealing position. Adjust the Pressure Cooker to high pressure and use the + or - buttons to set the duration to 6 minutes.

3. When the time is up, the cooker will beep. Turn the steam release handle to the Venting position with care (It will spurt out steam and water). You may open the lid after the Float Valve has gone down.
4. After removing the bay leaves, pour coconut milk. Process it until smooth and creamy with an immersion blender (or a normal blender). Season to taste. If the soup is too thick, thin it down with a little quantity of vegetable broth.

Broccoli Soup

Preparation time: 10 minutes | Total time: 30 minutes

Servings:4 | Difficulty Level: Easy

Nutritional Information:

Calories: 118 kcal, Protein: 9.5 g, Carbohydrates: 15.9 g, Fat: 2.6 g, Fiber: 2 g

Ingredients

- 1/4 cup of diced celery
- 1 1/2 cups of chopped broccoli
- 1/4 cup of chopped onion
- 2 cups of nonfat milk
- 1 cup of chicken broth; low-sodium
- 2 tablespoons of cornstarch
- 1 dash of pepper
- 1/4 teaspoon of salt
- 1/4 cup of grated Swiss cheese
- 1 dash of ground thyme

Instructions

1. In a saucepan, add the veggies and broth. Bring to a boil, then reduce to low heat and simmer until the veggies are soft, approximately 8 minutes. Combine the pepper, milk, salt, cornstarch, and thyme in a mixing bowl; stir in the cooked veggies.
2. Cook, stirring continuously, for approximately 5 minutes or until the soup has gently thickened and the mixture has just started to boil. Remove the pan from the heat. Stir in the cheese until it is completely melted.

☆ ☆ ☆ ☆ ☆

Sorrel Soup

Preparation time: 10 minutes | Total time: 40 minutes

Servings:8 | Difficulty Level: Easy

Nutritional Information:

Calories: 38 kcal, Protein: 2.2 g, Carbohydrates: 7.4 g, Fat: 0.7 g, Fiber: 3.1 g

Ingredients:

- 1 cup of chopped spinach
- 2 cups of chopped sorrel
- 1 chopped onion
- 2 cups of chopped cauliflower
- 8 cups of water
- 1 teaspoon of dried basil
- 4 cups of chopped tomatoes
- 1 tablespoon of avocado oil

Instructions:

In a pan, pour oil. On medium heat, add onion and roast it for 3-4 minutes. Then add the tomatoes, cauliflower, and dry basil. Add water and cook the soup for 10 minutes after. After that, add the sorrel and boil the soup for another 16 minutes. Allow time for the soup to cool before serving.

Main Courses Meat Recipes

Slow Cooker Dairy-Free Butter Chicken

Preparation time: 10 minutes | Total time: 6 hrs.

Servings:8 | Difficulty Level: Medium

Nutritional Information:

Calories: 304 Kcal, Protein: 28 g, Carbohydrates: 9 g, Fat: 18 g, Fiber: 2 g

Ingredients:
- 1-inch chopped knob of ginger
- 2 Tablespoons of Coconut Oil
- 1 tablespoon of garam masala
- 5 minced cloves of garlic
- 1 Tablespoon of cumin
- 2 teaspoons of ground turmeric
- 1 teaspoon of chili powder
- 1/2 teaspoon of ground pepper
- 1 teaspoon of sea salt
- 1/2 teaspoon of cayenne, optional
- 2 lb. skinless, boneless chicken breast; chunks
- 1/2 teaspoon of ground cinnamon
- 15 oz can of coconut milk; full fat
- 1 cinnamon stick1
- 5 oz can of tomato sauce
- 1 chopped yellow onion.
- 2 Tablespoons of lemon juice
- 1/4 cup of chopped cilantro
- 2 cups of frozen green beans; thawed, optional

Instructions:
1. Cook onion and garlic in oil in a wide skillet or saucepan until soft and aromatic for approximately 5 minutes. Add turmeric, fresh ginger, garam masala, chili powder, cumin, salt, cinnamon, pepper, and cayenne. Cook for 1-2 minutes more.

2. Add onion and garlic combination in a slow cooker. Then add tomato sauce, chicken, lemon juice, coconut milk, and cinnamon stick.
3. Cook on a high for 3 hours or on low for 6 hours, covered. Add the green beans when there's approximately an hour remaining in the cooking process.
4. Serve butter chicken with fresh cilantro and a lemon slice for squeezing over the cauliflower rice (normal rice).

Grilled Curry Chicken

Preparation time: 15 minutes | Total time: 25 minutes

Servings: 4 | Difficulty Level: Medium

Nutritional Information:

Calories: 212 Kcal, Protein: 37 g, Carbohydrates: 3 g, Fat: 5 g, Fiber: 3g

Ingredients:

- 1 1/2 lbs. skinless, boneless chicken breasts

Thai Curry Spice Blend

- 1/2 Tablespoon of onion powder
- 2 1/2 Tablespoons of curry powder
- 2-3 teaspoons of red pepper flakes; crushed
- 1 teaspoon of dried parsley
- 1 1/2 teaspoons of sea salt

Instructions:

1. To make the spice mix, combine the onion powder, curry powder, sea salt, crushed red pepper flakes, and parsley in a small bowl. Use as much spice mix as you need to coat each chicken breast. You may have some spice rub left over; store it in an airtight jar for later use. Just make sure you don't get any raw chicken juice on it.
2. Preheat a medium-hot indoor or outdoor grill. Lightly spray the grill grate, put the chicken on it, and cook for 5 to 6 minutes on each side or until the juices flow clearly. The time it takes to cook a chicken breast depends on its size.

Beefy Bake Casserole

Preparation time: 20 minutes | Total time: 50 minutes

Servings:4 | Difficulty Level: Medium

Nutritional Information:

Calories: 473 Kcal, Protein: 35 g, Carbohydrates: 55 g, Fat: 13 g, Fiber:6 g

Ingredients:

- 1/8 tsp of pepper
- 1 1/2 cups of gluten-free elbow macaroni, if needed
- 1 8 oz tomato sauce
- 1 lb. lean ground turkey, ground beef, or chicken
- 1 6 oz tomato paste
- 1/2-3/4 cup of celery finely; chopped
- 1 cup of water
- 1/2 cup of onion; finely chopped
- 1/4 tsp of chili powder
- 1/2 tsp of salt
- 1 cup of grated cheddar cheese/ more if desired
- 1 1/2 cups of frozen corn

Instructions:

1. Cook macaroni as per package instructions. Drain it and put it aside for 10-11 minutes. Brown the meat in the pan, eliminate fat, and add the onions and celery. Cook for approximately 5 minutes together. Except for the noodles, add all ingredients. Mix thoroughly. Add the noodles and toss them together gently. Sprinkle 1 cup of shredded cheddar cheese after pouring the macaroni into a 2 1/2-quart casserole and bake for 30 minutes at 35o degrees F.

Kung Pao Chicken

Preparation time: 10 minutes | Total time: 25 minutes

Servings:4 | Difficulty Level: Medium

Nutritional Information:

Calories: 340 Kcal, Protein: 27 g, Carbohydrates: 43 g, Fat: 8 g, Fiber:5 g

Ingredients:

- 4 minced cloves of garlic
- 1 lb. skinless, boneless chopped chicken breast; chunks
- 2 teaspoons of fresh ginger minced or grated
- 1 Tablespoon of sesame oil divided
- 3 cups of broccoli
- 1 chopped bell pepper orange, yellow, or red
- 2 chopped green onions
- crushed peanuts; for serving (optional)
- 2 cups of cooked brown rice; for serving

Sauce

- 1-2 Tablespoons of honey
- 1/4 cup of coconut aminos / soy sauce; low sodium /tamari
- 1/2-1 teaspoon of arrowroot powder; for thickening, optional
- 2 teaspoons of chili sambal Oelek paste/sriracha

Instructions:

1. To make the sauce, whisk together the ingredients in a small bowl.
2. In a large sauté pan or wok, heat 1/2 tbsp of sesame oil. When the pan is heated, add garlic, chicken, and ginger, and cook for 5-7 minutes or until the chicken is finished. Place the chicken on a platter. Toss the remaining oil, green onions, bell pepper, and broccoli in the same pan. Simmer for 5 minutes, or until broccoli is soft; add sauce and the chicken to the pan and cook

for another 2-3 minutes, or until sauce thickens. Remove from heat and set aside for 2-3 minutes.
3. Over brown rice, serve vegetables and kung pao chicken. For spicier, top with sriracha and crushed peanuts.

Chicken piccata with garlicky greens & new potatoes

Preparation time: 5 minutes | Total Time: 20 minutes

Servings: 2 | Difficulty Level: Easy

Nutritional Information:

Calories: 393 kcal, Protein: 41 g, Carbohydrates: 22 g, Fat: 13 g, Fiber: 13 g

Ingredients:

- 300g green beans; trimmed
- 200g new potatoes; halved or quartered
- 2 skinless chicken breasts
- 200g spring greens; shredded
- 1 tbsp of drained capers
- 3 tsp of olive oil
- 1 lemon; zested and juiced
- 100 ml chicken stock /water
- 1 tbsp of grated parmesan
- 2 small garlic cloves; sliced

Instructions:

1. In a large saucepan of boiling salted water, cook the fresh potatoes for 8-10 minutes or until cooked. For the final 3 minutes, add the spring greens and green beans. Drain and separate the greens from the potatoes.
2. While the potatoes are boiling, cut the chicken breasts lengthwise through the middle, leaving one side intact, so the breasts spread out like a book. Season with salt and pepper after brushing each with 1 tsp olive oil.
3. Cook chicken for 4 minutes on each side in a large frying pan over medium-high heat until browned. Pour in the capers, stock, lemon juice, and zest, and reduce the sauce slowly for

a few minutes. Cook for another minute after adding the cooked potatoes.
4. In a separate frying pan, heat the remaining 1 tsp oil and cook the garlic for 1 minute or until gently brown and aromatic. Add the drained greens in garlicky oil and mix to combine. Season with salt and pepper, then top with parmesan cheese and serve with the chicken and potatoes.

Apple Cider Vinegar Chicken

Preparation time: 1 hr. | Total time: 1 hour 15 minutes

Servings:3 | Difficulty Level: Medium

Nutritional Information:

Calories: 223 Kcal, Protein: 39 g, Carbohydrates: 1 g, Fat: 6 g, Fiber:3g

Ingredients:

- 2 Tablespoons of Italian seasoning
- 1/4 pound of skinless, boneless chicken breasts
- 1 Tablespoon of olive oil
- 1/4 cup of apple cider vinegar
- 1/2 teaspoon of ground pepper
- 1 teaspoon of sea salt

Instructions:

1. Mix the Italian seasoning, vinegar, salt, oil, and pepper in a mixing bowl. Place the chicken in a shallow dish or a 1-gallon plastic bag that can be sealed.
2. Refrigerate for about 1 hour or 12 hours after adding the marinade and tossing to coat. Remove the chicken from the marinade, shake off any excess, and discard the rest. Preheat a grill pan or a grill. Place the chicken on the grill once it's hot and cook for 5 minutes on each side or until it's cooked completely and no longer pink.
3. You may alternatively broil the chicken if you don't have a barbecue. Spray a broiler pan with cooking spray before lining it with foil. Put the chicken on a foil-lined baking sheet. Broil, keep an eye on it, so it doesn't burn. After approximately 5 minutes, flip the chicken. Cook for 10-15 minutes or until chicken is no longer pink and cooked through.
4. Enjoy the chicken right now, or chill it down, put it in storage containers, and preserve it for later.

☆ ☆ ☆ ☆ ☆

Boiled Chicken

Preparation time: 1 hr. | Total time: 1 hour 40 minutes

Servings:8 | Difficulty Level: Medium

Nutritional Information:

Calories: 186 Kcal, Protein: 16.3 g, Carbohydrates: 4.5 g, Fat: 11.1 g, Fiber:3 g

Ingredients

- 3 unpeeled carrots, smash into chunks
- 1 whole chicken (3 pounds)
- 2 stalks of celery, smash into chunks
- 1 large unpeeled halved onion, water to cover
- 1 tablespoon of whole peppercorns

Instructions

1. In a large saucepan, combine the onion, chicken, celery, carrots, and peppercorns, and cover with water. Then, boil, lower to low heat, and simmer for 90 minutes until the chicken flesh falls from the bone. Remove the chicken and set it aside to cool before shredding or chopping the flesh.

Vegetable Recipes II

Curried Chickpea Lettuce Wraps

Preparation time: 5 minutes | Total time: 10 minutes

Servings:2 | Difficulty Level: Medium

Nutritional Information:

Calories: 416 kcal, Protein: 14 g, Carbohydrates: 45 g, Fat: 23 g, Fiber: 18 g

Ingredients:

Chickpea Filling

- 1 chopped spring onion
- 1 can (about 400g) chickpeas; drained and rinsed
- 6 mint leaves
- 1 tsp of turmeric
- 1 tsp of cumin
- 1 chopped garlic clove
- 1 tbsp of olive oil
- 1 tbsp of sesame seeds
- 1 tsp of ground chili peppers
- 1 tbsp of flax seeds

Salad

- 12 basil leaves
- 1 avocado
- 2 chopped tomatoes
- 1 tsp of lime juice 1 chopped spring onion
- 6 Lettuce leaves; washed
- 1 chopped garlic clove
- 2 tbsp of crushed walnuts
- 1 chopped green pepper

Instructions:

1. Put chickpeas in a pan with a little water (approximately 1/4

cup), turmeric, and chili powder, and swirl to coat over medium-high heat (about 2-3 min)
2. Ensure no water is left in the pan before adding the other ingredients (garlic, olive oil, sesame seeds, onion, flax seeds, cumin, and mint leaves). Stir for approximately 1 minute, remove from heat, and cover with a lid.
3. Smash avocado and 1/2 diced tomato in a small bowl, add minced garlic, lime juice, and mix until smooth. To make it smoother, you may use a hand blender. Mix in the remainder of the salad components and additional salt to taste. For added nutrition and crunch, sprinkle crumbled walnuts over the top.
4. Arrange two tbsp. of chickpea filling and two tbsp. of salad in the center of a lettuce leaf. Rep approximately 5 times more and serve it.

Mediterranean Grilled Eggplant Salad

Preparation time: 30 minutes | Total time: 30 minutes

Servings: 6 | Difficulty Level: Easy

Nutritional Information:

Calories: 146 kcal, Protein: 3 g, Carbohydrates: 12 g, Fat: 11 g, Fiber: 5 g

Ingredients:

- 1 red bell pepper; medium
- 1/4 cup of pine nuts
- 1/2 cup of scallions; green part only
- 1 3/4 pound of unpeeled eggplant
- 3 tablespoons of olive oil
- 1 medium diced tomato
- 3/4 teaspoon of salt
- 2 tablespoons of fresh lemon juice
- 1/4 teaspoon of black pepper; freshly ground
- 1/2 cup of chopped fresh parsley
- 1/8 teaspoon of smoked paprika
- 2 tablespoons of chopped mint leaves
- 1/2 teaspoon of red pepper flakes; crushed

Instructions:

1. Toast pine nuts in a small heavy pan or skillet over medium heat for approximately 5 minutes, turning continuously until they become glossy and become golden brown in places. Because nuts burn quickly, keep a careful eye on them.
2. Red peppers should be halved and seeded. Cut the eggplant into 1-inch slabs lengthwise. Grill the veggies for approximately 15 minutes over medium heat on a charcoal or propane grill. When the grilled veggies are cool enough to handle, roughly chop them and place them in a medium

serving dish. Add scallion greens, tomato, mint, lemon juice, olive oil, parsley, salt, red pepper flakes, black pepper, and smoked paprika to the same dish. Serve warm or cold, tossing gently to mix ingredients.

Red Beet Borscht

Preparation time: 15 minutes | Total time: 1 hr. 15 minutes

Servings:6 | Difficulty Level: Medium

Nutritional Information:

Calories: 224 kcal, Protein: 6 g, Carbohydrates: 40 g, Fat: 6 g, Fiber: 10 g

Ingredients:

- 1 small chopped yellow onion
- 2 small peeled and shredded beets
- 1 large green bell pepper and a small chopped
- 2 tablespoons of olive oil
- 1 small, shredded head of green cabbage
- 1 8-ounce can of tomato sauce
- 4 medium peeled and shredded carrots
- 1/2 teaspoon of salt
- 3 medium peeled and halved potatoes
- 1/4 teaspoon of pepper
- 6 tablespoons of sour cream; for serving
- 4 bay leaves
- 2 cups of parsley, chopped
- 3 crushed garlic cloves

Instructions:

1. In a skillet, heat the olive oil over medium heat. Add bell pepper and onion. Sauté until the onion begins to become transparent.
2. Continue to Sautee after adding shredded carrots and beets for another 4 to 5 minutes. Stir in the tomato sauce until it is well combined. Heat for an additional 2 minutes before turning off the heat.
3. Add salt, shredded cabbage, and pepper in a separate big

saucepan. Bring to a boil with cold water, then cover and let simmer for approximately 20 minutes. Toss the halved potatoes into the cabbage pot. Cook after covering it until the potato is approximately halfway done.

4. Transfer the sauteed mixture to the cabbage-filled cooker. Add bay leaves, parsley, and smashed garlic. Turn off the heat after another 2 to 3 minutes of boiling.

Stir-Fried Asparagus with Bell Peppers and Cashew Nuts

Preparation time: 10 minutes | Total time: 20 minutes

Servings:4 | Difficulty Level: Easy

Nutritional Information:

Calories: 302 kcal, Protein: 9 g, Carbohydrates: 25 g, Fat: 20 g, Fiber: 4 g

Ingredients:

- 2 tablespoons of rice wine vinegar
- 3 tablespoons of vegetable broth; low sodium
- 2 tablespoons of hoisin sauce; gluten-free
- 3 tablespoons of balsamic vinegar
- 1 tablespoon of gluten-free, low, sodium tamari/soy sauce
- 1 teaspoon of toasted sesame oil
- 1 teaspoon of cornstarch
- 2 teaspoons of chili garlic sauce
- 1 cup of lightly chopped cashew nuts
- 2 teaspoons of sugar
- 1 tablespoon of high oleic sunflower oil /other neutral vegetable oil
- 2 cups of chopped fresh asparagus: 1-inch pieces
- 3 minced cloves garlic
- 2 bell peppers; stems removed deseeded and chopped; 1-inch pieces

Instructions:

1. To make the sauce, follow these steps: In a medium mixing bowl, combine the vinegar, sugar, broth, tamari, chili garlic sauce, hoisin sauce, and cornstarch. Stir everything together with a fork or a whisk until everything is thoroughly blended. Set it aside until you're ready to prepare the veggies. Bell

peppers and asparagus should be prepared ahead of time. Set aside after chopping into 1-inch pieces. Garlic should be minced and put aside.
2. Cashew nuts should be chopped. On medium heat, warm a wok or a big cast iron pan. Add cashew nuts and cook for 2 to 3 minutes, stirring, until gently browned in a wok/skillet over medium heat. Remove the wok/skillet from the heat and place it in a bowl until ready.
3. Add asparagus, sunflower/vegetable oil, and chopped garlic in a heated pan. Cook, stirring continuously, for 3 minutes over medium heat. Simmer for another 2 minutes after adding bell peppers, pour sauce over vegetables, and cook for another 2 to 3 minutes, or until sauce thickens.
4. Add cashew nuts and sesame oil and divide into four servings. Enjoy while it's still warm.

Vegan Tacos

Preparation time: 20 minutes | Total time: 20 mins

Servings: 4 | Difficulty Level: Medium

Nutritional Information:

Calories: 360 Kcal, Protein: 16.6 g, Carbohydrates: 32.6 g, Fat: 20.9 g, Fiber: 7.9 g

Ingredients:

- 2 tablespoons of tamari/soy sauce; reduced sodium
- 1 (16 ounces) package of drained, crumbled extra-firm tofu; patted dry
- 1/2 teaspoon of garlic powder
- 1 teaspoon of chili powder
- Pinch of salt
- 1/2 teaspoon of onion powder
- 1/2 cup of fresh salsa
- 1 tablespoon of olive oil; extra-virgin
- 2 cups of iceberg lettuce, shredded
- 1 ripe avocado
- 8 corn /flour tortillas; warmed
- 1 tablespoon of vegan mayonnaise
- Pickled radishes; for garnish
- 1 teaspoon of lime juice

Instructions:

1. In a medium mixing bowl, combine garlic powder, tamari/soy sauce, tofu, chili powder, and onion powder. In a large nonstick pan, heat the oil over medium-high heat. Cook, stirring periodically until the tofu mixture is well browned; it will take about 8 to 10 minutes.
2. In a small bowl, mash the avocado with lime juice, mayonnaise, and salt until smooth. In tortillas, serve the taco

"meat" with salsa, avocado crema, and lettuce. If preferred, serve with pickled radishes on top.

Sweet Potatoes with Swiss Chard

Preparation time: 10 minutes | Total time: 30 mins

Servings: 4 | Difficulty Level: Medium

Nutritional Information:

Calories: 169 Kcal, Protein: 3.3 g, Carbohydrates: 19.7 g, Fat: 9.1 g, Fiber: 4.2 g

Ingredients:

- 2 diced cloves of garlic
- 1 chopped red onion
- 1 bunch of Swiss chard; chopped, tough stems removed
- 2 medium sweet potatoes; wedges or rounds

Dressing:

- 1 tsp of maple syrup
- 2 Tbsp of red wine vinegar
- 1 Tbsp of grainy Dijon mustard
- sea salt and pepper; to taste
- 1/2 cup of toasted pecans

Instructions:

1. Cook the onion for a few minutes over medium heat with 1/4 cup of water before adding the garlic. Add potatoes and continue to sauté until nearly tender. Add the Swiss chard and a bit more water, then cover with the lid. Steam until soft. Meanwhile, make the dressing by whisking together the ingredients in a bowl. Transfer the Swiss chard and potatoes to a mixing bowl with the dressing and toss to incorporate. If preferred, top with pecans and serve warm or cold.

☆ ☆ ☆ ☆ ☆

Stuffed Peppers

Preparation time: 25 minutes | Total time: 55 mins

Servings: 4 | Difficulty Level: Medium

Nutritional Information:

Calories: 216 Kcal, Protein: 7.7 g, Carbohydrates: 34.9 g, Fat: 5.9 g, Fiber: 5.7 g

Ingredients:

- 1 medium chopped onion
- 3 large red peppers; half lengthwise, seeds removed
- 8 oz sliced mushroom
- 2 chopped cloves of garlic
- 1 1/2 cups of cooked brown rice/ quinoa
- 8 sun-dried tomatoes, soaked in hot water, roughly chopped
- 1 15 oz can have drained and rinsed kidney or other beans
- 2-3 roughly chopped large leaves of Swiss chard
- 1/3 cup of raw cashews; finely chopped
- 1-2 cups of pasta sauce/tomato sauce

Instructions:

1. Preheat the oven to 375 degrees Fahrenheit. For 5 minutes in boiling water, parboil the peppers.
2. In a big sauté pan with a small amount of water, sauté the onions. Add mushrooms and garlic and continue to simmer until nearly tender. Add and cook chard and beans until wilted. Add spaghetti sauce, sun-dried tomatoes, and 1 1/2 cups of rice. To mix, stir everything together.
3. Fill the pepper "cups" to the brim and garnish with chopped cashews. Cook for 20-25 minutes, covered until heated through. Remove the foil and cook the cashews for another 5-10 minutes.

☆ ☆ ☆ ☆ ☆

Sautéed greens with fennel

Preparation time: 15 minutes | Total time: 20 mins

Servings: 6 | Difficulty Level: Medium

Nutritional Information:

Calories: 41.5 Kcal, Protein: 1.6 g, Carbohydrates: 9.9 g, Fat: 0.2 g, Fiber: 3.6 g

Ingredients:

- 1 small head of roughly chopped fennel (about 1 cup)
- Pinch of salt and pepper
- 2 tablespoons of soft coconut oil
- 1 large head of Swiss chard, green or rainbow, chopped (6 cups)
- Pinch of ground cinnamon
- 2 tablespoons of balsamic vinegar
- 1/4 teaspoon of dried thyme
- 2 tablespoons of golden raisins

Instructions:

1. In a medium-sized pan, melt the coconut oil. Add fennel to the pan and simmer, stirring regularly, for 8-10 minutes or until softened. In the same pan, add the greens. Toss and cook for 4 minutes or until wilted.
2. Add balsamic vinegar, thyme, golden raisins, and cinnamon. Toss the coat evenly. Cook for a minute or two or until the vinegar bubbles and caramelize. Season to taste with salt and pepper.
3. Serve at room temperature or warm.

☆ ☆ ☆ ☆ ☆

Desserts

Pumpkin Balls

Preparation time: 10 minutes | Total time: 10 minutes

Servings: 4 | Difficulty Level: Easy

Nutritional Information:

Calories: 222 Kcal, Protein: 8.4 g, Carbohydrates: 17.3 g, Fat: 15.2 g, Fiber: 4.4 g

Ingredients:

- 1 oz chia seeds
- 4 oz crushed pumpkin seeds
- 1 teaspoon of honey
- 5 chopped dates

Instructions:

1. In a mixing bowl, combine all ingredients and stir until smooth. Make balls out of the mixture and keep them refrigerated for up to 4 days.

☆ ☆ ☆ ☆ ☆

Mango Pudding

Preparation time: 10 minutes | Total Time: 10 minutes

Servings: 2 | Difficulty Level: Easy

Nutritional Information:

Calories: 395 kcal, Protein: 15.4 g, Carbohydrates: 51.8 g, Fat: 15.2 g, Fiber: 17.4 g

Ingredients:

- 1 cup of plain Greek yogurt/ unsweetened
- 1 peeled mango; blended
- 1 teaspoon of fresh mint
- 3 oz chia seeds

Instructions:

1. Combine the plain yogurt and chia seeds in the serving glasses. The yogurt is topped with pureed mango and fresh mint.

☆ ☆ ☆ ☆ ☆

Strawberry Shortbreads

Preparation time: 20 minutes | Total time: 30 minutes

Servings: 4 | Difficulty Level: Easy

Nutritional Information:

Calories: 120 Kcal, Protein: 3 g, Carbohydrates: 32 g, Fat: 11 g, Fiber: 3 g

Ingredients:

- 1/2 teaspoon of vanilla essence
- 400g strawberries
- 1 1/2 tablespoons of icing sugar
- 100g coconut oil
- 200g thick coconut yogurt
- 80g banana
- 225g flour; gluten-free
- 50g sugar

Instructions:

1. Preheat the oven to 180 degrees Celsius/160 degrees Celsius fan. Place half of the strawberries in a bowl and sprinkle with a teaspoon of icing sugar. While you're making the shortbread, put it in the fridge. Combine the sugar, coconut oil, and banana. Mix in the flour and make the dough. On a floured board, roll out the dough and cut out 16 circles using a pastry cutter. Cook for 12 minutes or until golden brown. Allow time for cooling. Combine the remaining icing sugar, the coconut yogurt, and the vanilla extract. Just before serving, put everything together. Place one shortbread circle on a plate, spread a couple of heaped teaspoons of coconut yogurt mixture over it, top with strawberries, and top with another shortbread circle. Using icing sugar, dust the cake.
2. Repeat with the remaining shortbread, then top with the remaining strawberries.

☆ ☆ ☆ ☆ ☆

Gingerbread Dessert Hummus

Preparation time: 5 minutes | Total time: 10 minutes

Servings: 6 | Difficulty Level: Easy

Nutritional Information:

Calories: 236 kcal, Protein: 5 g, Carbohydrates: 40 g, Fat: 7 g, Fiber: 5 g

Ingredients:

- 1/4 cup of Almond Butter; all natural
- 1 13.5 ounces rinsed and drained Can of Chickpeas
- 2 tablespoons of Blackstrap Molasses
- 3 tablespoons of Maple Syrup
- 2 teaspoons of Cinnamon Powder
- 1 teaspoon of Vanilla Extract
- 3/4 teaspoon of Ginger Powder
- 1 pinch of Salt
- 1/4 teaspoon of Ground Cloves

Instructions:

1. In a food processor, combine all of the ingredients. Pulse until the chickpeas are integrated and the hummus has a smooth texture. Fill a dish with the dessert hummus and serve with gingerbread cookies, apples, or anything else you want. Serve.

☆ ☆ ☆ ☆ ☆

Watermelon Pizza

Preparation time: 10 minutes | Total Time: 10 minutes

Servings: 4 | Difficulty level: Easy

Nutrition Information:

Calories: 150 Kcal, Protein: 10 g, Carbohydrates: 21 g, Fat: 4 g, Fiber: 2 g

Ingredients:

- 2 large round slices of watermelon about 1 inch thick
- 3/4 cup of Low fat or fat-free plain Greek yogurt
- 1 teaspoon honey
- 1 tsp vanilla extract
- 1 cup fresh strawberries, sliced
- 1 cup fresh blackberries, sliced in half (You may use fresh blueberries if blackberries are unavailable. You can also use bananas or raspberries with, or instead, of strawberries)
- A handful of fresh mint leaves, rough chopped, optional

Instructions:

1. Mix well with yogurt, honey, and vanilla in a bowl. Divide yogurt in half, and spread equal amounts on each watermelon round. Decorate each watermelon round with berries and sprinkle with mint leaves if using. Cut each watermelon round into 8 slices and serve.

Chocolate Avocado Pudding

Preparation time: 5 minutes | Total Time: 5 minutes

Servings: 4 | Difficulty Level: Easy

Nutritional Information:

Calories: 324 kcal, Protein: 6 g, Carbohydrates: 34 g, Fat: 23 g, Fiber: 13 g

Ingredients:

- 1/3 cup of raw cacao powder
- 2 large avocados; chilled
- 2 tsp of vanilla extract
- 1/2 cup of full-fat coconut milk
- 1/3 cup of maple syrup

Optional Toppings

- sea salt
- Hazelnuts; chopped

Instructions:

1. Remove the pit from the avocados and cut them in half. Fill a food processor halfway with flesh. Add remaining ingredients and stir well. Scrape down sides as required until the mixture is smooth and creamy. Check to see if you need to add any more sweetness. In four serving dishes, divide the chocolate avocado pudding. Serve with your preferred garnishes, such as hazelnuts & sea salt.

Apple Chips

Preparation time: 10 minutes | Total time: 3 hours

Servings: 2 | Difficulty Level: Easy

Nutritional Information:

Calories: 113 Kcal, Protein: 1 g, Carbohydrates: 30 g, Fat: 0 g, Fiber: 5 g

Ingredients:

- 1/2 tsp. of cinnamon
- 2 apples; thinly sliced
- 2 tsp. of honey

Instructions:

1. Toss apples with honey and cinnamon in a large mixing bowl. Arrange apples in a single layer in an air fryer basket in batches (some overlap is okay). Cook at 350°F for 12 minutes, turning after every 4 minutes.

☆ ☆ ☆ ☆ ☆

Pineapple Sorbet

Preparation time:50 minutes | Total time: 55 minutes

Servings:4 | Difficulty Level: Medium

Nutritional Information:

Calories: 73 Kcal, Protein: 0.5 g, Carbohydrates: 19.5 g, Fat: 0.1 g, Fiber: 1.2 g

Ingredients:

- 2 cups of chopped pineapple
- 1 teaspoon of fresh mint
- 2 tablespoons of liquid honey

Instructions:

1. Blend the pineapple until it is completely smooth. Mix in the liquid honey and the mint. The mixture should be stirred. Fill the silicone molds halfway with the mixture and freeze for 40 minutes. Then take the mixture from the molds into the processor and blend until smooth. Fill the serving dishes with dessert.

Kiwi Sorbet

Preparation time: 15 minutes | Total Time: 15 minutes

Servings: 2 | Difficulty Level: Easy

Nutritional Information:

Calories: 93 kcal, Protein: 1 g, Carbohydrates: 23 g, Fat: 1 g, Fiber: 5 g

Ingredients:

- 1 lime juiced
- 3 kiwis

Instructions:

1. Peel and slice the kiwis into rounds. Place the slices on a parchment-lined baking sheet and freeze until firm, for about 2-3 hours.
2. Add the fresh lime juice to the frozen kiwi slices in a food processor or high-powered blender. Pulse fruit until it achieves a sorbet-like consistency. You'll have to wipe the sides down a few times to attain uniformity.
3. Serve right now or freeze for later. If you freeze it, it will take 15 to 20 minutes to defrost enough to consume.

Fresh Fig & Banana Smoothie

Preparation time: 5 minutes | Total Time: 5 minutes

Servings: 2 | Difficulty Level: Easy

Nutritional Information:

Calories: 365 kcal, Protein: 9 g, Carbohydrates: 74 g, Fat: 7 g, Fiber: 9 g

Ingredients:

- 1 1/2 cups of unsweetened almond milk
- 1 frozen banana
- 3-4 fresh figs; washed & stems removed and halved
- 1 teaspoon of vanilla extract
- Handful of ice
- 1 tablespoon of ground flaxseeds; optional

Instructions:

1. In a blender, combine all ingredients and mix until creamy and smooth. Serve right away! This dish also works nicely with frozen fresh figs.

☆ ☆ ☆ ☆ ☆

Almond Butter Avocado Fudgsicles

Preparation time: 30 minutes | Total time: 4 hours 30 minutes

Servings: 8 | Difficulty Level: Medium

Nutritional Information:

Calories: 218 kcal, Protein: 4 g, Carbohydrates: 12 g, Fat: 20 g, Fiber: 8 g

Ingredients:

Almond Butter Avocado Fudgsicles

- 2/3 cup of Cacao Powder
- 2 large Avocados, ripe
- 1 cup of full-fat Coconut Milk from a can
- 2 teaspoons of Liquid Stevia
- 2-3 tablespoons of maple syrup/honey; to taste
- Crushed almonds & flaky sea salt; for topping
- 1 teaspoon of Vanilla Extract
- Chocolate shell; for dipping
- 1/3 cup of Almond Butter

Chocolate Shell

- 1 teaspoon of Liquid Stevia
- 1 tablespoon of maple syrup/honey; to taste
- 1/2 cup of Coconut Oil; melted
- 1/4 cup of Cacao Powder

Instructions:

Almond Butter Avocado Fudgsicles

1. Combine the cacao powder, avocados, vanilla extract, coconut milk, and liquid stevia (maple syrup/honey) in a food processor or high-powered blender. Blend until the mixture is smooth and creamy. Adjust the sweetness to your liking if necessary. In the chocolate fudge mixture, stir in the almond

butter. Do not overmix the ingredients.
2. Fill popsicle molds halfway with almond butter fudge mixture. Make sure the fudge mixture goes to the bottom of the molds by tapping them on the counter a few times. Put a popsicle stick in the center of each slot and cover the popsicles with the lid (if you have one).
3. Place them in the freezer for at least 4 hours, preferably overnight. After the molds have been frozen, run them under cold Water for a few minutes to help the popsicles come out more readily. Remove the popsicles from the mold, coat them with chocolate (if desired), then sprinkle with sea salt and crushed almonds (optional). Serve and have fun!

Chocolate Shell

1. Combine the cacao powder, melted coconut oil, and stevia (honey /maple syrup) in a large mixing bowl. Adjust the sweetness to your liking if necessary.
2. Place the popsicles on parchment paper to harden after dipping them in the melted chocolate mixture. Serve and have fun!

Easy Roasted Fruit

Preparation time: 30 minutes | Total Time: 30 minutes

Servings: 4 | Difficulty Level: Medium

Nutritional Information:

Calories: 199 kcal, Protein: 2.8 g, Carbohydrates: 39.7 g, Fat: 5.9 g, Fiber: 4.5 g

Ingredients:

- 1 1/2 cups of fresh blueberries
- 2 peaches, peeled & sliced
- 2 tablespoons of honey
- 1/8 teaspoon of ground cinnamon

Instructions:

Preheat the oven to 350 degrees Fahrenheit. In a baking dish, layer sliced peaches and blueberries. Cinnamon & brown sugar are sprinkled on top.

Bake for approximately 20 minutes at 350 degrees F, then reduce to a low broil setting and broil for about 5 mins or until bubbling. Allow to cool before serving, then cover and refrigerate.

☆ ☆ ☆ ☆ ☆

Guava Smoothie

Preparation time: 30 minutes | Total time: 5-7 minutes

Servings: 2 | Difficulty Level: Easy

Nutritional Information:

Calories: 166 kcal, Protein: 3.9 g, Carbohydrates: 3 g, Fat: 1.4 g, Fiber: 7.8 g

Ingredients:

- 1 cup of chopped guava, seeds removed
- 1 cup of finely chopped baby spinach
- 1 tsp of fresh ginger, grated
- 1/2 medium-sized peeled and chopped mango
- 1 banana, peeled and sliced
- 2 cups of Water

Instructions:

Cut the guava in half after peeling it. Wash it after scooping out the seeds. Set aside after cutting into small pieces. Under cold running water, thoroughly rinse the baby spinach. Drain well and rip into tiny pieces. Put it aside. Peel and cut the banana into tiny pieces. Put it aside. Cut the mango into tiny pieces after peeling it and put it aside. Mix the guava, banana, ginger, baby spinach, and mango in a juicer and process until smooth. Gradually drizzle in the Water and mix until everything is smooth and creamy. Before serving, transfer to serving glasses and chill for 20 minutes. Enjoy!

Orange Ginger Turmeric Smoothie

Preparation time: 30 minutes | Total Time: 0 minutes

Servings: 2 | Difficulty Level: Easy

Nutritional Information:

Calories: 79 kcal, Protein: 2 g, Carbohydrates: 19 g, Fat: 1 g, Fiber: 4 g

Ingredients:

- 1large, chopped carrot
- 2 navel oranges; quartered and peeled
- 1-inch ginger piece; peeled
- Pinch of black pepper
- 1-inch turmeric piece; peeled

Instructions:

In a high-powered blender, combine all the ingredients, including 1 cup of ice cubes. Blend on high speed until completely smooth. For a more juice-like smoothie, add up to a cup of Water.

☆ ☆ ☆ ☆ ☆

Turmeric Apple Cider Ginger Gummies

Preparation time: 15 minutes | Total Time: 4 hours 15 minutes

Servings: 8 | Difficulty Level: Medium

Nutritional Information:

Calories: 5 kcal, Protein: 0 g, Carbohydrates: 2 g, Fat: 0 g, Fiber: 0 g

Ingredients:

- 3 tablespoons of honey (maple syrup)
- 1 tablespoon of freshly grated ginger
- 1 teaspoon of ground turmeric
- 3 1/2 tablespoons of grass-fed unflavored gelatin powder
- 1 1/2 cups of apple cider vinegar
- 1 1/2 cups of water; divided

Instructions:

1. In a skillet over medium heat, combine honey, grated ginger, ground turmeric, apple cider vinegar, and 1 cup water. Let the mixture simmer for a few minutes. After straining the grated ginger bits out, turn off the heat in the skillet.
2. Add the gelatin powder gradually while stirring the remaining 1/2 cup water in a small bowl. Whisk the gelatin mixture until it is completely dissolved before adding it to the apple cider vinegar liquid.
3. Fill a 10" x 7" glass baking pan with the mixture. Wrap in plastic wrap, then refrigerate until firm (for 4 hours / overnight). Once set, cut into 3-inch squares that are enough to serve or keep for a week in the refrigerator.

Herbal Teas

Peppermint Tea

Preparation time: 10 minutes | Total Time: 15 minutes

Servings: 4 | Difficulty level: Easy

Nutritional Information:

Calories: 34.2 kcal, Protein: 0.1 g, Carbohydrates: 0 g, Fat: 0 g, Fiber: 0g

Ingredients:

- 1/2 cup dried Peppermint Leaf
- 4 cups of hot water

Instructions:

1. Set Water to boil. Once boiling, add peppermint leaves and remove them from the heat. Cover and let rest for at least 5 minutes. Strain, serve, and enjoy.

Almond Tea

Preparation time: 10 minutes | Total Time: 5 minutes

Servings: 2-3 | Difficulty level: Easy

Nutritional Information:

Calories: 40 kcal, Protein: 1.5 g, Carbohydrates: 1.4 g, Fat: 3 g, Fiber: 2 g

Ingredients:

- 5 Tbsp. Almond powder
- 1 cup Water
- 1 tsp. Cinnamon

Instructions:

1. Boil water with all ingredients. Serve warmly.

☆ ☆ ☆ ☆ ☆

Chamomile Tea

Preparation time: 10 minutes | Total Time: 5 minutes

Servings: 2 | Difficulty level: Easy

Nutritional Information:

Calories: 1 kcal, Protein: 0 g, Carbohydrates: 0.4 g, Fat: 0 g, Fiber: 0.7 g

Ingredients:

- 2 cups Water
- 3 teaspoons Dried Chamomile

Instructions:

1. Bring water to a boil in a pot over high heat. As soon as the water begins to boil, turn off the heat and add dried Chamomile. Keep the lid on for one minute. Pour the chamomile tea through a strainer into the teacups, stir it up, and serve.

Turmeric Tea

Preparation time: 10 minutes | Total Time: 20 minutes

Servings: 4 | Difficulty level: Easy

Nutritional Information:

Calories: 26.8 kcal, Protein: 0.1 g, Total Carbs: 6.8g, Dietary Fiber: 0g, Total Fat: 0g

Ingredients:

- 1 handful of cilantro; chopped
- 32 oz boiling water
- 1 Tbsp of olive oil
- 1/2 Tbsp of turmeric powder
- 1 garlic clove; peeled & crushed
- 2 lemons; juiced
- 1 Tbsp of fresh ginger; thinly sliced
- 1 orange; juiced (or 1 1/2 tbsp of honey)
- 5 peppercorns; whole

Instructions:

1. Heat water in a saucepan and then stir in the remaining ingredients. Serve hot.

Herbal Tea

Preparation time: 10 minutes | Total Time: 10 minutes

Servings: 2 | Difficulty level: Easy

Nutritional Information:

Calories: 37 kcal, Protein: 0.4 g, Carbohydrates: 7 g, Fat: 0.7 g, Fiber: 0.3 g

Ingredients:

- 5 cup water
- 1/4 tsp clove powder
- 1 tsp fennel seeds
- 5 green cardamoms
- 10 mint leaves
- 1/4 tsp ginger powder

Instructions:

1. In a saucepan, bring water to a boil. Add all the herbs and boil for 2 minutes. Turn off the flame and cover the saucepan for 5 minutes so the herbs can infuse. Strain the tea in another saucepan and bring it to a boil. Serve hot.

☆ ☆ ☆ ☆ ☆

Lemon Grass Tea

Preparation time: 10 minutes | Total Time: 10 minutes

Servings: 2 | Difficulty level: Easy

Nutritional Information:

Calories: 1.8 kcal, Protein: 0 g, Carbohydrates: 0.5 g, Fat: 0 g, Fiber: 0 g

Ingredients:

- 2 sticks of lemongrass
- 1 lemon
- 1 1/2 cup water

Instructions:

1. In a small saucepan, add water and add lemongrass. Bring the water to a boil and lower the flame. Let it simmer for 5 to 6 mins. Turn off the flame and strain the tea into your cup. Squeeze a lemon in the tea to enhance flavor. Enjoy your tea.

☆ ☆ ☆ ☆ ☆

Peach Tea

Preparation time: 10 minutes | Total Time: 10 minutes

Servings: 2 | Difficulty level: Easy

Nutritional Information:

Calories: 0 kcal, Protein: 0 g, Carbohydrates: 1 g, Fat: 0 g, Fiber: 0 g

Ingredients:

- 2 tsp dried peach bits
- 1 lemon
- 1 1/2 cup water

Instructions:

1. In a small saucepan, add water and dried peach bits. Bring the water to a boil and lower the flame. Let it simmer for 5 to 6 mins. Turn off the flame and strain the tea into your cup. Squeeze a lemon in the tea to enhance flavor. Enjoy your tea.

Jasmine Tea

Preparation time: 10 minutes | Total Time: 15 minutes

Servings: 2 | Difficulty level: Easy

Nutritional Information:

Calories: 56.2 kcal, Protein: 0 g, Carbohydrates: 17 g, Fat: 0 g, Fiber: 0 g

Ingredients:

- 1 tsp dried jasmine flowers
- 1 1/2 cup water
- Few mints leaves

Instructions:

1. In a saucepan, put water, jasmine tea, and mint leaves. Bring the water to a boil. Boil for 2 minutes and turn off the stove. Cover the saucepan and let the tea infuse. After 10 minutes, turn on the flame and boil it. As soon as the tea boils, strain it into your cup and enjoy it.

Herbs

Italian Seasoning

Preparation time: 10 minutes | Total time: 5 minutes

Servings: 6 | Difficulty Level: Easy

Nutritional Information:

Calories: 17.5 kcal, Protein: 0.8 g, Carbohydrates: 3.9 g, Fat: 0.3 g, Fiber: 1.7 g

Ingredients:

- 1tbsp of Dried Thyme
- 2 tbsp of Dried Oregano
- 1 tbsp of Dried Rosemary
- 1 tbsp of Dried Marjoram
- 2 tbsp of Dried Basil

Instructions:

1. Combine oregano, Basil, garlic powder, onion powder, parsley, and black Pepper. Store it in an airtight jar.

☆ ☆ ☆ ☆ ☆

All-Purpose No-Salt Seasoning Mix

Preparation time: 10 minutes | Total Time: 5 minutes

Servings: 10 | Difficulty Level: Easy

Nutritional Information:

Calories: 20.7 kcal, Protein:1 g, Carbohydrates: 3.7 g, Fat: 1 g, Fiber: 1.5 g

Ingredients:

- 1 1/4 teaspoon ground thyme
- 1 teaspoon ground mace
- 1 tablespoon garlic powder
- 1 1/2 teaspoons dried parsley
- 1 1/2 teaspoons dried Basil
- 1 teaspoon ground black pepper
- 1 teaspoon onion powder
- 1 1/4 teaspoon dried savory
- 1/4 teaspoon cayenne pepper
- 1 teaspoon dried sage

Instructions:

Mix Basil, garlic powder, parsley, thyme, savory, onion powder, mace, sage, cayenne Pepper, and Black Pepper, and reserve it in a covered jar.

Garlic-Herb Seasoning

Preparation time: 10 minutes | Total Time: 5 minutes

Servings: 6 | Difficulty Level: Easy

Nutritional Information:

Calories: 5.2 kcal, Protein: 0.2 g, Carbohydrates: 1 g, Fat: 0.2 g, Fiber: 0.4 g

Ingredients:

- 1 tsp Powdered lemon rind
- 2 tsp Garlic powder
- 1 tsp Oregano
- 1 tsp Basil

Instructions:

1. In a processor, combine ingredients. Store rice grains to avoid clumping in a sealed jar.

Poultry Seasoning

Preparation time: 3 minutes | Total time: 3 minutes

Servings: 5 | Difficulty Level: Easy

Nutritional Information:

Calories: 13.5 kcal, Protein: 0.4 g, Carbohydrates: 2.9 g, Fat: 0.3 g, Fiber: 0.5 g

Ingredients

- 1 tsp black pepper: ground
- 2 tbsp ground sage: dried
- 2 tsp dried marjoram
- 2 tsp dried thyme

Instructions

1. In a small bowl, combine all ingredients. Add this blend to an airtight jar. Good to use for one year.

☆ ☆ ☆ ☆ ☆

Anti-Inflammatory Oil

Preparation time: 10 minutes | Total time: 10 minutes

Servings:4 | Difficulty Level: Easy

Nutritional Information:

Calories: 116 kcal, Protein: 0.2 g, Carbohydrates: 1.7 g, Fat: 12.9 g, Fiber: 1 g

Ingredients:

- 1 tablespoon of dried thyme
- 1/4 cup of olive oil
- 1 peeled garlic clove
- 2 tablespoons of dried rosemary

Instructions

1. Close the lid on the can after adding all of the ingredients. Refrigerate oil for 1-2 days.

Sambal Oelek

Preparation time: 5 minutes | Total time: 10 minutes

Servings:6 | Difficulty Level: Easy

Nutritional Information:

Calories: 9 kcal, Protein: 0.1 g, Carbohydrates: 2 g, Fat: 0 g, Fiber: 0.1 g

Ingredients:

- 1 tablespoon of salt
- 2 tablespoons of rice vinegar
- 1 pound of red chili peppers; stems removed

Instructions

1. In a food processor or equivalent grinder, combine all of the ingredients. A Molcajete is an excellent choice for this. Grind until you get a coarse paste. If you want to, strain off some of the extra liquid. Cover and place in a jar. Keep it refrigerated until you're ready to use it.

Hot Ketchup

Preparation time:10 minutes | Total time:15 minutes

Servings:4 | Difficulty Level: Easy

Nutritional Information:

Calories: 19 kcal, Protein: 0.9 g, Carbohydrates: 4 g, Fat: 0.2 g, Fiber: 1.2 g

Ingredients:

- 1 minced jalapeno pepper
- 1 teaspoon of dried Basil
- 2 cups of chopped tomatoes
- 1 minced chili pepper
- 1 teaspoon of minced garlic

Instructions

1. Pour the tomatoes into the pot after blending them into a smooth paste. Add garlic, dried Basil, jalapeño pepper, and chili pepper. Bring the ketchup to a boil in a saucepan.

☆ ☆ ☆ ☆ ☆

Mustard Dressing

Preparation time:10 minutes | Total time:10 minutes

Servings:4 | Difficulty Level: Easy

Nutritional Information:

Calories: 58 kcal, Protein: 3.6 g, Carbohydrates: 3.3 g, Fat: 3.6 g, Fiber: 1.3 g

Ingredients:

- 3 tablespoons of lemon juice
- 3 tablespoons of mustard
- 1 egg, beaten.

Instructions

1. The egg should be whisked. Add lemon juice and mustard. Combine the dressing ingredients well.

☆ ☆ ☆ ☆ ☆

Measuring Conversions

There are two widely employed measuring schemes in nutrition: Metric and US Customary. **Dry Measure Equivalent**

3 teaspoons	1/2 ounce	1 tablespoon	14.3 grams
2 tablespoons	1 ounce	1/8 cup	28.3 grams
4 tablespoons	2 ounces	1/4 cup	56.7 grams
5 1/3 tablespoons	2.6 ounces	1/3 cup	75.6 grams
8 tablespoons	4 ounces	1/2 cup	113.4 grams
12 tablespoons	6 ounces	3/4 cup	.375 pound
32 tablespoons	16 ounces	2 cups	1 pound

Weight (mass)	
Metric (grams)	**US contemporary (ounces)**
14 grams	1/2 ounce
28 grams	1 ounce
85 grams	3 ounces
100 grams	3.53 ounces
113 grams	4 ounces
227 grams	8 ounces
340 grams	12 ounces
454 grams	16 ounces or 1 pound

Volume (liquid)	
Metric	US Customary
.6 ml	1/8 tsp
1.2 ml	1/4 tsp
2.5 ml	1/2 tsp
3.7 ml	3/4 tsp
5 ml	1 tsp
15 ml	1 tbsp
30 ml	2 tbsp
59 ml	2 fluid ounces or 1/4 cup
118 ml	1/2 cup
177 ml	3/4 cup
237 ml	1 cup or 8 fluid ounces
1.9 liters	8 cups or 1/2 gallon

Oven Temperatures	
Metric	US contemporary
121° C	250° F
149° C	300° F
177° C	350° F
204° C	400° F
232° C	450° F

www.ingramcontent.com/pod-product-compliance
Lightning Source LLC
Chambersburg PA
CBHW050248120526
44590CB00016B/2265